30 Days to the Parables

A Devotional Commentary

Bill Curtis

with Cassie Martin

Seed Publishing Group, LLC
Timmonsville, South Carolina

30 Days to the Parables: A Devotional Commentary

Copyright © 2021 by Bill Curtis with Cassie Martin

Published by:
Seed Publishing Group
2570 Double C Farm Ln
Timmonsville, SC 29161
seed-publishing-group.com

Edited by:
Bill Curtis, Ph.D.
Dwayne Milioni, Ph.D.

All rights reserved. No part of this book may be reproduced or transmitted in any form or by any means, electronic or mechanical, including photocopying and recording, or by any information storage or retrieval system, except as may be expressly permitted in writing by the publisher. Requests for permission should be addressed in writing to Seed Publishing Group, LLC; 2570 Double C Farm Lane; Timmonsville, SC 29161.

Scripture quotations are from The Holy Bible, English Standard Version® (ESV®), copyright © 2001 by Crossway, a publishing ministry of Good News Publishers. Used by permission. All rights reserved.

To order additional copies of this resource visit www.seed-publishing-group.com.

Library of Congress Control Number: 2020931347

ISBN-13: 978-0-9985451-6-5

Printed in the United States of America

To the Elders of Cornerstone:

Thank you for the gracious privilege to use my gifts in service to the Lord at Cornerstone.

Thank you for your faithful service to our Lord, and for helping me shoulder the load for ministry and mission, on both joyous and grievous days.

"I thank my God in all my remembrance of you, always in every prayer of mine for you all making my prayer with joy, because of your partnership in the gospel from the first day until now. And I am sure of this, that he who began a good work in you will bring it to completion at the day of Jesus Christ. It is right for me to feel this way about you all, because I hold you in my heart, for you are all partakers with me of grace."

Philippians 1:3-7a

Contents

Foreword xi

The Kingdom of God

Day 1 Parable Introduction 1
    Mark 4:11-12
Day 2 Lost Things Part One 7
    Luke 15:1-32
Day 3 Lost Things Part Two 13
    Luke 15:1-32
Day 4 Wheat and the Weeds 19
    Matthew 13:24-30; 36-43
Day 5 New Wineskins 25
    Matthew 9:14-17
Day 6 The Rich Man and Lazarus 31
    Luke 16:19-31
Day 7 Pharisee and the Tax Collector 39
    Luke 18:9-14
Day 8 The Great Banquet 47
    Luke 14:12-24

Kingdom Residents

Day 9 The Narrow Door 55
    Luke 13:22-30
Day 10 Hidden Treasure 61
    Matthew 13:44-46
Day 11 Tower/Army 69
    Luke 14:25-33
Day 12 Lampstand 77
    Matthew 5:14-16
Day 13 Soils 83
    Mark 4:1-20
Day 14 Mustard Seed 89
    Luke 13:18-30

Day 15 Kind Money Lender 95
    Luke 7:36-50
Day 16 The Talents 101
    Matthew 25:14-30

Kingdom Fruits

Day 17 Banquet Seats 111
    Luke 14:1-11
Day 18 Two Foundations 119
    Luke 6:46-49
Day 19 Two Sons..125
    Matthew 21:28-32
Day 20 Dishonest Manager 133
    Luke 16:1-13
Day 21 Early and Late Workers Part One 141
    Matthew 20:1-16
Day 22 Early and Late Workers Part Two 147
    Matthew 20:1-16
Day 23 Rich Fool 153
    Luke 12:13-21
Day 24 Good Samaritan Part One...................................161
    Luke 10:25-37
Day 25 Good Samaritan Part Two.................................. 169
    Luke 10:25-37
Day 26 Unforgiving Servant..175
    Matthew 18:21-35
Day 27 Persistent Friend Part One..................................181
    Luke 11:1-13
Day 28 Persistent Friend Part Two 189
    Luke 11:1-13
Day 29 Faithful Servants 197
    Luke 12:35-40
Day 30 Persistent Widow 203
    Luke 18:1-8
Finding L.I.F.E. in Jesus! 211

Foreword

Some of the best-known stories in all the Bible are the parables of Jesus. Some of the most misunderstood texts in all the Bible are the parables of Jesus. Because both aforementioned statements are true, every Christian needs a skilled guide to lead them toward a clear understanding of these profoundly important biblical passages. Dr. Bill Curtis is that guide.

Get the parables of Jesus wrong, and you will be confused about the nature of Christ's kingdom. Get the parables wrong, and you will be vulnerable to moralism and legalism. Get the parables wrong, and you will struggle to fully understand the earthly ministry of Jesus. Conversely, getting the parables right will help you get the gospel of Christ and the Christ of the gospel right.

The format of this book will make it a beneficial tool for so many different people. To the pastor, this devotional commentary will offer you keen insights into important texts, but it will warm your heart as you struggle through days and seasons of spiritual dryness. For the church member searching for a sound devotional, this book will give you access to a seasoned pastor and a sharp theologian. You will get the meat of the Word, without having to look up obscure theological terms, cloaked in technical, academic language. To the Bible college student or seminarian, this book will serve as a model for you. Use all the faculties and gifts God has given you to serve his church by presenting the Bible with clarity and creativity—two things Dr. Curtis does remarkably well.

Foreword

It is good for us to remember, as well, that the impact of the parables reaches far beyond the formal teaching of a worship service or a Sunday School class. I've lost track of how many times I've used the parables in counseling. For the one who needs to behold the love of God for struggling sinners, is there a more powerful story than the parable of the lost son in Luke 15? For the one struggling with the whole concept of biblical forgiveness (being forgiven and forgiving others), is there a more potent text in all of Scripture than Matthew 18:21-35? As you will find within the pages of this excellent book, the words of Jesus carry eternal wisdom. Sometimes the words of the Lord confront; sometimes they comfort. But, they are always good! Understand these truths, so that you might wield them for the glory of Christ and the good of his people.

– Dr. Jason D. Wredberg
Redeemer Bible Church
Minnetonka, MN

Day 1

Parable Introduction

Mark 4:11-12

A man looked at his old, brown couch with concern. It was 10 years past its prime, and the weight of countless guests had taken its toll. The fabric was still intact although it bore some stains from past Super Bowl parties. The frame was strong and solid, but the cushions had begun to sag. He knew that it was time for a new couch.

When the new couch was scheduled to be delivered, the man realized that it was time to dispose of his old one. He thought about taking it to the dump, but it was still in decent shape. He was sure that someone could get some more use out of it. So, with the help of a neighbor, he took the couch down to the street and set it in front of his building. He made a hand-written sign with bold, red letters that read, "Free!" Then, he went back inside.

You can imagine his surprise when the couch was still there the following day. And the day after that. A week later he stood on the sidewalk looking at his forlorn couch. Then he made a decision to try something different. He removed his original sign and replaced it with another. It read, "$10." Again, he went back into his apartment. The next day when he left for work, the couch was gone. Someone had stolen it in the night.

The Kingdom of God

> *Reject God long enough, and he will stop giving you opportunities to experience forgiveness and restoration.*

What you have just read is called a parable. TED author Chris Anderson defines parables as "stories carefully designed as metaphors," meaning they carry a "moral or spiritual lesson."[1] Parables take events from everyday life and infuse them with deeper meaning. The story above is about more than a guy who cannot seem to give his couch away. The deeper meaning is connected to the sudden twist in the story, when the couch is stolen the moment a monetary amount is linked to it. The principle of this parable is simple: People want things that add value to their lives. When the couch was free, it had no value. As a result, it couldn't add value to someone else. But when there was a price attached, that was different. Now, it was valuable enough to be stolen.

The parables of Jesus take a variety of different forms. Some are short (parable of the Mustard Seed) and others are long (parable of the Two Sons). Some are based on true stories (parable of the Rich Man and Lazarus), while others are invented (parable of the Dishonest Manager). Many of the parables are natural analogies, which explore everything from hidden treasures to construction projects. You are about to embark on a 30-day study of the parables of Jesus. These stories contain some of the most memorable images and sayings from Jesus' teaching ministry.

Have you ever wondered why Jesus used parables so often in his teaching (Mk 3:2)? You're not alone—his disciples wondered the same thing. Mark records that conversation for us. "And when he [Jesus] was alone, those around him with the twelve asked him about the parables (Mk 3:10)." As you might imagine, the parables had the potential to be confusing to Jesus' listeners.

I imagine his followers were even more confused when he answered their question: "To you has been giv-

1. Anderson, C. 2017. *TED Talks: The Official TED Guide to Public Speaking*. First Mariner Books.

Day 1

en the secret of the kingdom of God, but for those outside everything is in parables, so that 'they may indeed see but not perceive, and may indeed hear but not understand, lest they should turn and be forgiven (Mk 3:11-12).'" To fully understand this response, we must note that Jesus was quoting from Isaiah 6:9-10. In that text, God was calling Isaiah to be his prophet. But his ministry would be a challenging one. The people of Israel were living in rebellion against God. They claimed to be worshipers of Yahweh, and even participated in temple rituals, yet they were fully syncretistic, meaning they also worshiped the pagan gods of the Canaanites and participated in their hedonistic practices. Despite the warning of God's prophets, the people continued headlong into rebellion. Because of this, God promised to punish his people. The northern nation of Israel fell to the Assyrians in 722 BC (while Isaiah was alive in Judah), while the southern nation of Judah fell to the Babylonians in 586 BC. Because of his people's wickedness, God shut the ears and eyes of his people to the message of the prophets. It's not that God was unwilling to reveal his truth—lots of Israelites in those days were faithful followers of God and his law. But there is a principle about parables here that we cannot miss: Reject God long enough, and he will stop giving you opportunities to experience forgiveness and restoration.

The Israel that Jesus was born into had changed much since the days of Isaiah—at least in practice. The Pharisees and other religious leaders had created a hyper-legalistic system designed to protect the people from returning to an idolatrous lifestyle. Yet, while the outward appearance of the people was conformed to the Old Testament law, the internal condition of their hearts remained unchanged. The arrival of Jesus, Israel's Messiah, initiated a brand new covenant between God and the people he created, both Jew

The arrival of Jesus, Israel's Messiah, initiated a brand new covenant between God and the people he created, both Jew and Gentile.

The Kingdom of God

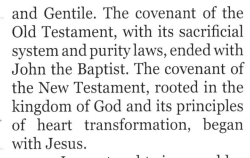

Parables provide gospel realities to receptive hearts, but hide gospel realities from hardened hearts.

and Gentile. The covenant of the Old Testament, with its sacrificial system and purity laws, ended with John the Baptist. The covenant of the New Testament, rooted in the kingdom of God and its principles of heart transformation, began with Jesus.

Jesus taught in parables for strategic reasons. First, parables were designed to help people visualize the kingdom of God on earth, while simultaneously exposing the flaws of works-based, religious cultures. Those who believed in Jesus were "given the secret of the kingdom of God." As Kingdom residents, they were called to embrace a life that was counter-intuitive and counter-cultural. They learned that in God's kingdom greatness comes from serving, receiving comes from giving, and living comes from dying. And, as Kingdom residents, the word of God was no longer written on stone tablets but upon their hearts (Jer 31:33). These followers had the benefit of hearing Jesus' interpretation of the parables and receiving the rich truth that they contained.

Those who rejected Jesus, on the other hand, were continuously confused by the parables of Jesus. The second reason Jesus taught in parables was to reveal authentic seekers, while hiding truth from religious skeptics like the Pharisees, scribes, and Sadducees. Rather than serving as a roadmap to faith, the parables served instead as roadblocks to faith. It's important to understand at this point that Jesus wasn't using parables to keep people away from faith and salvation. By God's gracious design, **parables provide gospel realities to receptive hearts, but hide gospel realities from hardened hearts.**

In truth, all of Scripture works like this. The Bible is God's word, written. "All Scripture is breathed out by God and profitable for teaching, for reproof, for correction, for training in righteousness (2 Tim 3:16)." The Bible contains

Day 1

everything we need for spiritual life and godliness, but it is received through our knowledge of God (2 Pet 1:3). That knowledge is available to anyone who hears the word of God and receives it as truth by faith (Rom 10:5-17). Those who reject the good news of the kingdom will find nothing in the parables but confusing words and images. But those who receive the good news of the kingdom will find great joy and help in the parables. So, enjoy the next 30 days. God has some great kingdom truths waiting for you!

Those who receive the good news of the Kingdom, however, will find great joy and help in the parables.

The Kingdom of God

Food for Thought — The parables aren't Jesus' version of Aesop's fables. There isn't a "moral" to the story. Instead, the parables of Jesus provide real-life descriptions of the kingdom of God on earth. There are principles to be learned for sure. In fact, most of Jesus' parables reveal one, simple, Kingdom principle. But the goal of these parables isn't to improve our morals; they aren't self-help remedies. Instead, the goal is the spiritual transformation of our hearts and minds (Rom 12:1-2). With that in mind, how do you want this study to impact your life over the next 30 days?

Faith in Action — Take some time today to design a 30-day plan for this study. Each day takes about 15-20 minutes to read the chapter and reflect on its application. Look at your calendar and decide when you will do this study each day. Will you read each devotion early in the morning? On your lunch break? When you get home? Before you go to bed? I am always a fan of having my devotions first thing in the morning. I want to have the chance to reflect on God's truth all day. Often, God takes the things I read in the morning and allows me to share them later in the day with people I encounter. If I read before bed, sleep often robs me of the benefits of personal reflection. Still, I'd rather you read at night than not at all. Got your schedule of reading set for the month? Let's go!

Prayer

Spend some time in prayer today. Ask God to help you enjoy and value the time you spend studying the parables. Thank him for revealing himself through his word and for promising to complete the work of transformation he started in you. He knows exactly what you need to gain from this study, so ask him to make that clear as you study each parable.

Lost Things
Part One

Luke 15:1-32

There are few things more frightening than the thought of losing something we value. Several years ago my family and I were on vacation, and we stopped at a coffee shop for a break. I took my laptop inside to check on our itinerary while we had some coffee. When we were finished, we hopped into the car and headed up the interstate. About thirty minutes later, I had that sickening feeling that comes from realizing that you've forgotten something; I had forgotten my laptop! I turned the car around and raced back to the coffee shop. When I arrived, there was no sight of my laptop, and the employees said they hadn't seen it.

    I was crushed. I was in the final stages of writing *Engaging Exposition*, and I knew that I hadn't backed up my files in months. The work of nearly three years was gone. Of course, I was most upset at myself. Self-inflicted stupid is the worst kind of injury. That was one of the very few times in my life that I actually felt panic. I had not only lost my book manuscript, but also many other important projects. In despair, I laid my head on the counter and wept.

    In my grief, I turned and looked back into the storage room that was adjacent to the counter. I saw racks filled with bags of coffee, cups, and filters, along with a

The Kingdom of God

> *Some things are so valuable to us that if we lose them, we will do whatever it takes to find them again.*

stack of empty packing boxes. As I stared at the pile of boxes, I noticed what looked like a small piece of black canvas poking out from behind it. I wondered – could that be my laptop case? I asked the guy behind the counter what it was, and he told me that it was nothing. At this point I began to suspect that something was amiss. So, I asked him to go look, and he pulled out my missing laptop bag! The guy at the coffee shop was planning to steal it.

Here's what's weird, though. I was so overjoyed at finding my lost laptop and having it back in my possession, that I didn't even care that he had planned to steal it. Immediately, my fear and panic subsided, and I was filled with joy. I had rarely felt that kind of relief in my whole life. At that moment, I realized something important about the kingdom principle in today's parable: Some things are so valuable to us that if we lose them, we will do whatever it takes to find them again.

When Jesus was involved in his ministry on earth, he was passionate about finding lost things, too. He often spent time with the people on the fringes of society—tax collectors, criminals, and prostitutes—the people who needed him most. Because he did this, he often faced ridicule and rebuke from the religious establishment of the Jews: the Pharisees, Sadducees, and scribes. This is the setting as Luke 15 begins: "Now the tax collectors and sinners were all drawing near to hear him. And the Pharisees and the scribes grumbled, saying, 'This man receives sinners and eats with them (vv. 1-2).'"

When Jesus heard their complaints, he proceeded to tell them three parables designed to confront their judgmental hypocrisy. The first story he told was about a farmer who had 100 sheep (vv. 3-7). In Jesus' day, that was a large enterprise. One day the farmer did a quick inventory and realized that one of his sheep was missing. Despite the fact that he had 99 others, the farmer went in search of that

Day 2

one sheep. This makes sense if you think about it. After all, if you don't care about losing one sheep, pretty soon you won't have any. So he expended his time, energy, and resources to locate it. He was filled with joy when he located it, and he called his friends and neighbors to celebrate with him.

Then, Jesus told another story about a woman who lost part of her wedding dowry (vv. 8-9). In Jesus' day, a woman was given a dowry by her parents when she got married. The dowry belonged to her, not to her husband. A woman was given the dowry in the event that her husband chose to divorce her. It would ensure that she would not be left destitute. As a result, a woman's personal dowry was priceless to her. In this story, a woman loses one of her 10 dowry coins. It's night when she discovers her loss, but she doesn't wait until morning to begin her search. She lights a lamp in a panic and begins to scour the house. She is overwhelmed with joy when she finds it, and she, too, calls her friends and neighbors to celebrate with her.

Then, Jesus told the point of the story (vv. 7, 10): the angels and residents of heaven celebrate every time someone places their faith in Jesus for salvation. Just like the farmer who found his lost sheep and the woman who found her lost dowry coin, all of heaven rejoices when a single lost person is found.

Jesus then told his third story—the parable of the lost son (vv. 17-32). This story is about a father who had two sons. The older son was living in a seemingly loving, obedient relationship with his father. But the younger son was headstrong and rebellious, always chafing under his father's authority. As a result, the youngest son took his inheritance and departed to seek what he imagined to be freedom. Over time, he spent all of his money partying, gambling, and living recklessly. When a famine hit his country, he discovered that all of his friends

> *All of heaven rejoices when a single lost person is found.*

The Kingdom of God

had vanished along with the food. He was totally alone.

Finally, he found a job working for a farmer, and he was tasked with feeding the pigs. As a Jewish man, even a wayward one, this was the ultimate indignity, but his survival depended on it. He was resigned to eating the scraps left by the pigs. What had looked like freedom turned out to be worse than living in his father's domain.

> *What had looked like freedom turned out to be worse than living in his father's domain.*

Then, and only then, did he come to his senses. In a singular moment of clarity, he realized that his father's hired workers lived in far better conditions than he did. Aware of his own rebellious choices, he made a pact with himself. He said, "I will arise and go to my father, and I will say to him, 'Father, I have sinned against heaven and before you. I am no longer worthy to be called your son. Treat me as one of your hired servants (vv. 18-21).'" With this plan in mind, he headed home.

When he neared the family farm, his father saw him walking up the road. He ran to meet his son and threw his arms around him. As he had planned, the young son confessed his sins to his father. Before he could even finish speaking, his father called to a nearby servant and told him to bring a new set of clothes, his signet ring, and some new shoes. Then, he commanded that they have a great homecoming celebration! Can you imagine the young man's surprise at his father's reaction? He came home expecting to be a servant, yet he was reinstated to his position as a son. As the story ended, his father said, "For this my son was dead, and is alive again; he was lost, and is found (v. 24)." In each of the three parables, Jesus was reinforcing his mission – "to seek and to save the lost (Lk 19:10)."

> *In each of the three parables, Jesus was reinforcing his mission – "to seek and to save the lost."*

Day 2

Food for Thought The Pharisees could not understand why Jesus received and dined with the disreputable because they didn't understand his mission to seek and save the lost. They believed the kingdom of God belonged only to the pious, and they failed to recognize their own sin. How does Jesus' parables in Luke 15 confront their hypocrisy? What does each story reveal about the nature of God's pursuing grace?

Faith in Action Try to remember a time when you thought you had lost something of great value to you. How did you feel while it was lost? How did you feel when you found it? Spend some time today reflecting on your status in God's kingdom – still lost or rescued by Jesus. If you have been found, take a few moments to imagine the celebration in heaven when Jesus rescued you. Thank God for welcoming you into his family with all the inheritance rights of a child, and look for opportunities to share your story today. If you are not sure whether you have been saved by Jesus, please read "Finding L.I.F.E. in Jesus" at the end of this book.

Prayer As you have your prayer time today, think about someone in your sphere of influence who needs to have a personal relationship with Jesus. Ask God to work in their hearts to draw them to Christ and to give you an opportunity to share the gospel with them.

Day 3

Lost Things
Part Two

Luke 15:1-32

When we left our young prodigal yesterday, he was enjoying an amazing homecoming feast. He had returned home hoping to be received as a hired servant, but he was welcomed by his father as a long-lost son. Not everyone was happy, however. Remember his older brother? He was about to throw a massive temper tantrum.

As our story resumes, the father's oldest son was farming in one of the fields nearby. Apparently he didn't see his brother return, so when he headed up to the house on a break he was surprised to hear the distant sounds of music and dancing. Curious, he shouted out to a nearby servant, "Hey, what's going on?" The servant responded with excitement, "Your brother has come, and your father has killed the fattened calf, because he has received him back safe and sound (v. 27)."

The news stopped the older brother in his tracks as a tidal wave of emotions broke over him. Unlike his father, the primary emotion he felt wasn't joy—it was anger (v. 28). To understand his visceral response, we must understand a few things about the Jewish laws of primogeniture. The firstborn son was the most important son in a family. As firstborn, he had several advantages over his broth-

The Kingdom of God

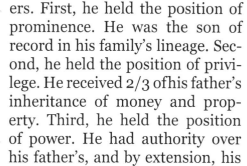

> Jesus came to rescue people who were lost and to reclaim worshipers for the glory of his father.

ers. First, he held the position of prominence. He was the son of record in his family's lineage. Second, he held the position of privilege. He received 2/3 of his father's inheritance of money and property. Third, he held the position of power. He had authority over his father's, and by extension, his family's affairs. This was a responsibility he would shoulder until he passed it down to his own firstborn son. As you can see, the oldest son in this story had always been the favored child. Then his little brother had acted out and thrown a wrench into the family dynamic. He didn't mind his brother leaving, of course, although it did put a dent in the family's net worth. Still, his brother took his own share of the inheritance when he left, so it hadn't affected his personal bottom-line. Life had settled into a new normal during the months he had been away. In fact, in some ways life had been easier—his brother always had been a rebel.

Now his wasteful, slacker of a brother was back, and his father was throwing him a party? He felt the rage boiling up in his heart as he clenched his jaw and stared towards the house. He didn't understand his father's logic, but he understood one thing—he would never go to a party to celebrate the return of his brother. Just then, he saw someone walking towards him from the house. He knew from the gait and the pace that it was his father. "Sheesh," he whispered under his breath.

He listened quietly as his father urged him to come inside and celebrate the return of his brother, but his mind was elsewhere; he couldn't hear a word his father was saying. Finally, it was his turn to give the speech he'd been rehearsing in his mind. "Look, these many years I have served you, and I never disobeyed your command, yet you never gave me a young goat, that I might celebrate with my friends. But when this son of yours came, who has devoured your property with prostitutes, you killed the fat-

Day 3

tened calf for him (vv. 29-30)!" The final words burst from his lips with a passion born of deep-seated bitterness.

Honestly, he couldn't believe the depth of his father's grace. Maybe he was getting soft in his old age. At this rate, he might give away the whole farm. He continued to fume—he wasn't about to yield a single denarii of his inheritance to his little brother, that's for sure. He knew why his little brother came home—he was out of money. Well, too bad. He should have thought about that before he took off in the first place. Suddenly, he was aware that his father was speaking to him again. This time he listened, "Son, you are always with me, and all that is mine is yours. It was fitting to celebrate and be glad, for this your brother was dead, and is alive; he was lost, and is found (vv.31-32)." Jesus didn't tell us the final response of the father's oldest son. Something tells me that he sighed, shook his head, and headed back out to the fields to work.

At this point, we have to revisit the introductory verses of Luke 15: "Now the tax collectors and sinners were all drawing near to hear [Jesus]. And the Pharisees and the scribes grumbled, saying, 'This man receives sinners and eats with them.'" It was in response to this sentiment that Jesus told the parables of the lost sheep, the lost coin, and the lost son. The Pharisees and other Jewish religious leaders were infuriated by Jesus' willingness to spend time with people they deemed to be "sinners." After all, the Pharisees believed that they were free from this label because of their religious lifestyles (Lk 18:9-14).

In reality, they had lost sight of the reason why God created the nation of Israel in the first place. When God entered into a covenant relationship with Abraham he said, "And I will make of you a great nation, and I will bless you and make your name great, so that you will be a blessing. I will bless those who bless you, and him who dishonors you I will curse, and in you all families of the earth shall be blessed (Gen

God wants to transform my heart by reminding me of my daily need for grace.

The Kingdom of God

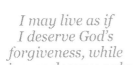

> *I may live as if I deserve God's forgiveness, while sinners deserve only judgment.*

12:2-3)." Did you catch that? God's plan to redeem the nation of Israel, by sending Messiah to be their Savior, was never limited by God to Israel alone. Matt Rogers notes, "The story of God gathering a worshiping people is never meant to end with the nation of Israel. Instead, it is meant to extend to the very ends of the earth through Israel. Since God desires his glory to fill the earth, and since the nations are scattered over the entire earth, the best way to have his glory fill the earth is to gather a people from every tribe, tongue, and nation. The people of the world could know God by becoming a part of his covenant promises to the nation of Israel (*Aspire: Transformed by the Gospel, Part One*)."

The Pharisees and other religious leaders had long ceased viewing their mission as one of international outreach. In fact, they despised Gentile sinners, especially the Romans, and refused to engage them with the hope of a covenant relationship with God. Ultimately, they came to despise Jewish "sinners" as well, believing that they would be defiled by contact with them. They would much rather judge sinners than see them reclaimed by God as obedient worshipers (Mt 7:1-5).

Yet, here was Jesus, God's Son, spending time with the lowest in Jewish society—tax collectors and sinners. One day, Jesus was eating at the house of Levi, the reformed tax collector and future apostle. Notice the response of the Pharisees and their scribes, "Why do you eat and drink with tax collectors and sinners?" Jesus replied, "Those who are well have no need of a physician, but those who are sick. I have not come to call the righteous, but sinners to repentance (Lk 5:27-32)." Here, Jesus provides us with the motive behind his ministry and the principle of today's parable: Jesus came to rescue people who are lost and to reclaim worshipers for the glory of his father. Like the father of the prodigal son, he found great joy in reaching those who seemed unreachable.

Day 3

The response of the older brother in this parable is the response of the Pharisees and the other religious leaders in Jesus' day. And sometimes, it's my response as well. It's easy as a follower of Jesus to become comfortable with my circle of Christian friends, impervious to the spiritual needs of the people around me. There is a deeper sin here that we must pause to consider regardless of how painful it may be. The Pharisees in Jesus' day believed that they deserved the blessings of the father because of their position and performance. They failed to recognize their own sin and desperate need for God's mercy. As a result, they didn't feel compelled to care about the people around them who were also in need of God's mercy.

I'm capable of the very same feelings and motives. Like the older brother in this parable, I may be angered by the actions of "sinners" and actually hope for their destruction. I may live as if I deserve God's forgiveness, while sinners deserve only judgment. I may act as if I'm incapable of sinning, while judging those whom I deem to be less spiritual than myself. All of these emotions are wicked, sinful, and full of pride.

Instead, God wants to transform my heart by reminding me of *my* daily need for grace. I was the wandering son who rebelled against the gracious authority of the Father. I was the sheep incapable of finding my way back to the safety and care of the Shepherd. I was the coin worth a midnight search and a joyous celebration. When I see my position before God accurately, I am equipped to embrace the compassion of Jesus in relation to other sinners. I can stop judging them and start loving them as I have been loved. I can share the hope of Jesus' saving grace with them, and I can rejoice when any sinner is reclaimed as a worshiper for the glory of God.

> When I see my position before God accurately, I am equipped to embrace the compassion of Jesus in relation to other sinners. I can stop judging them and start loving them as I have been loved.

The Kingdom of God

Food for Thought — When the older brother witnessed his father's joy over his prodigal brother's return, he was angry. He felt his brother deserved punishment, not a party. Only he had been obedient to his father's rules, but his wayward brother was now receiving the celebration he felt he deserved. Reflect on your heart before God. Do you bargain or reason with God based on your religious performance? Do you expect to be compensated with tangible blessings for obedience or service to God? Do you begrudge blessings to those who don't seem to "do" as much as you do for God?

Faith in Action — Throughout the day, pay attention to your attitudes and actions towards others. If you begin to rely on your own performance or good deeds for right status in God's kingdom, confess. Remind yourself of who you were: the lost sheep, the lost coin, the prodigal son; in need of rescuing, finding, and restoring. If you begin, in pride, to compare your spiritual performance or activity to others, confess. Rejoice in the grace you have been shown, and ask for help to share that same grace with others. When we remember who we were and what Jesus did for us, we can sing and share his "Amazing Grace! How sweet the sound that saved a wretch like me. I once was lost, but now I'm found – was blind, but now I see!"

Prayer

When you pray today, ask the Holy Spirit to reveal any points of pride or spiritual superiority in your heart, and then confess them to the Lord. He is faithful and just to forgive (1 Jn 1:9). Ask to share in Jesus' compassion for the lost, and pray, by name, for people you know who need the saving forgiveness that God offers through Christ.

Day 4

Wheat and the Weeds

Matthew 13:24-30; 36-43

Imitations are never as good as the real thing. I'm a huge fan of the music of Elvis Presley. Occasionally, I'll take in a show by an Elvis impersonator; it's never as good as the original. Similarly, I'm a huge fan of Hellman's mayonnaise (immediately, I can hear the cries from my friends who prefer Dukes!) For me, no other brand will do. The problem with counterfeits is that they often look the same as the original—until you look more closely. Then, all you will find is an imposter.

In today's parable, Jesus told the story of a tragic event in the life of a farmer. It was time to plant his wheat crop, so he took his good seed and sowed it into his fields. However, we soon discover that he had an enemy who wanted his crop to fail. While his workers slept, the farmer's enemy and his workers snuck into the fields and sowed tares among the wheat. This was a common occurrence in the Roman empire. If you had a hated rival, or wanted to drive up the cost for your crops by causing the crops of others to fail, you would sow "darnel" into the fields. Darnel was a weed that looked exactly like wheat. There was just one problem—it was a counterfeit. It looked like wheat on the outside, but when you opened the head of the plant it

The Kingdom of God

We who have been rescued can take comfort in Jesus' words and look with anticipation for the end of the age. We will shine forever in the kingdom of God, as we experience an eternity of joy and peace.

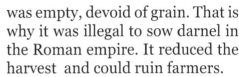

was empty, devoid of grain. That is why it was illegal to sow darnel in the Roman empire. It reduced the harvest and could ruin farmers.

Now, back to the story. Days went by before the farmer's workers discovered the treachery. When they did, they rushed to the house of the farmer. The questions spilled out of them. "Didn't you plant good seed? Where did all of these weeds come from? Should we go and pull them out of the fields?" Finally, the farmer quieted them. After some reflection, he began to answer their questions. "An enemy has done this to me. Regardless, we cannot attempt to pull out the weeds. If we do, we'll pull up the good wheat at the same time, and my losses will be even greater. We'll wait until the harvest, and then we'll separate the wheat from the weeds. We'll sell the good crop and burn the darnel."

When Jesus explained this parable, he identified the significance of each part of the story. He said,

> The one who sows the good seed is the Son of Man. The field is the world, and the good seed is the sons of the kingdom. The weeds are the sons of the evil one, and the enemy who sowed them is the devil. The harvest is the end of the age, and the reapers are angels. Just as the weeds are gathered and burned with fire, so will it be at the end of the age. The Son of Man will send his angels, and they will gather out of his kingdom all causes of sin and all law-breakers, and throw them into the fiery furnace. In that place there will be weeping and gnashing of teeth. Then the righteous will shine like the sun in the king-

dom of their Father. He who has ears, let him hear (vv. 37-43).

As you can see, this parable reveals key differences between believers and unbelievers, both in identity and outcome. First, Jesus explains that wheat and weeds are distinctive in their identity.

Believers are identified as the "good seed" in the parable. They have been planted by God, meaning that God has empowered them by the Spirit to hear, understand, and believe the word of God (1 Cor 1:18-2:16). They are adopted into God's kingdom with the rights and blessings of sonship. As they are transformed into the likeness of Christ, believers bear spiritual fruit for God's glory. Many of the parables we will study in the coming days explore the identity of Kingdom residents and the resulting spiritual fruit.

Unbelievers are the "bad seed" or the "weeds" in the parable. They are identified as "sons of the evil one (v. 38)." God's enemy Satan has sown them into the kingdom of God. To unbelievers, "the word of the cross is folly (1 Cor 1:18)." Whether they outwardly despise the truths of God's word or inwardly seek their own justification through good works, unbelievers lack a saving understanding of the gospel. As a result, some bear obvious fruits of unrighteousness – unrepentant sin and evil works of the flesh (Gal 5:19-21). Others may appear to bear good fruit. They may perform religious activities, treat people with kindness, and give charitably to important causes. However, while humanity looks at outward appearances, God looks at the heart (1 Sam 16:7). Just as the farmer could identify grain-producing wheat from empty weeds, God knows the children of his kingdom.

At the end of the age, Jesus will send his angels to "harvest" the world. When the wheat and the weeds are gathered and inspected, their identities will be exposed. In his explanation of the parable, Jesus reveals the second difference between believers and unbelievers: outcome.

The Kingdom of God

> As they are transformed into the likeness of Christ, believers bear spiritual fruit for God's glory.

Believers look forward to the day of harvest. Jesus paints a beautiful picture of their outcome: "the righteous will shine like the sun in the kingdom of their Father (v. 43)." In calling believers "the righteous," Jesus offers peace to believers while we await the harvest. We know that there is none righteous on earth – not even one (Rom 3:10). Our best deeds are tainted by sinful pride, comparison, judgmentalism, and wrong motivations. We are wholly incapable of earning the title of "the righteous." To be called "righteous" is to be identified with the righteousness of Jesus. Therefore, we who have been rescued can take comfort in Jesus' words and look with anticipation for the end of the age. We will shine forever in the kingdom of God, as we experience an eternity of joy and peace.

Those who have yet to understand and believe the word of God often lack security when they consider death or the possibility of an after-life. To quell their fears, they preach the "I'm enough gospel" to themselves: "I am good enough – smart enough, kind enough, rich enough, generous enough – to stand before any deity who may confront me." The next few days of our study together will explore several of the means through which unbelievers seek to clothe themselves in their own righteousness. But, those who have not been clothed in Christ's righteousness will experience a tragic outcome at the final harvest: eternal separation from God in hell, a place of sorrow and torment.

Even our best efforts fall woefully short of crafting a saving righteousness for ourselves. Weeds can desperately try to look like wheat, but they remain empty of grain. We need a new identity. We need to be re-planted. We need to be gifted God's righteousness through faith in the finished work of Jesus. It is then that we can be secure in a new outcome.

Day 4

Food for Thought Take a few moments to read Revelation 21: 1-8. Here, the Apostle John describes his Spirit-inspired vision of the end of the age, and again we see two outcomes in this passage. While those who are not God's children will find their portion in hell (v. 8), those who are God's children will dwell securely with him, and "God himself will be with them as their God. He will wipe away every tear from their eyes, and death shall be no more, neither shall there be mourning, nor crying, nor pain anymore, for the former things have passed away (vv. 3-4)."

Faith in Action How does living with eternity in mind shape our perspective on this life's circumstances? How should it shape our interactions with those who may not know Christ? While we await our promised future, God desires to transform us and produce the fruits of the Spirit in our lives (Gal 5) for his glory and for the furthering of his kingdom.

Prayer Today, rejoice that God has planted you in his kingdom fields and clothed you in his righteousness. Rest in his transforming grace, and ask him to use you to bless those around you and to share the hope that you have with those who have yet to believe in Jesus.

Day 5

New Wineskins

Matthew 9:14-17

I keep an old Dodge truck on my farm. It's in pretty good shape, but it needs new seals in the engine, and the price tag for that repair is $1,500. Since I don't want to spend that money on my truck, I keep pouring an $80 bottle of sealant into the engine every six months. It's a "quick fix" that allows my truck to run, but the systemic problem is still present; my truck needs new seals—period. I still remember the time I lost a bunch of weight on the Atkins diet. Once my body got into ketosis, the weight just fell off. I stopped the diet when I reached my goal. I loved the new me! About six months later, however, I had regained most of my weight. Why? The Atkins diet is a "quick fix." It allowed me to lose weight on the surface without addressing the systemic problems—I didn't have good eating or exercise habits.

We may treat our spiritual lives in a similar way. We run to God to get a "quick fix" when we have a crisis. We may go to church a few times, say some prayers, and maybe even give an offering, all in the hopes that God will bail us out. When we do that, we're simply attempting to patch a little bit of God onto our beggars rags—to pour a little bit of God into our broken lives. In essence, we want enough of God to ease our conscience but not enough to

The Kingdom of God

change our hearts. It reminds me of the words of Wilbur Rees in his 1971 book *$3.00 Worth of God*:

> I would like to buy $3 worth of God, please.
> Not enough to explode my soul or disturb my sleep, but just enough to equal a cup of warm milk
> or a snooze in the sunshine.
>
> I don't want enough of God to make me love a black man
> or pick beets with a migrant.
> I want ecstasy, not transformation.
> I want the warmth of the womb, not a new birth. I want a pound of the Eternal in a paper sack.
> I would like to buy $3 worth of God, please.

When we live like this, we are missing the whole point of the gospel. In today's parables, Jesus uses the imagery of the "quick fix" to highlight the transformative purpose and power of the gospel.

One day, Jesus and his disciples were approached by some of John the Baptist's friends and followers. They asked Jesus a curious question: "Why do we and the Pharisees fast, but your disciples do not fast (v. 14)?" This was a big deal to them. When we read the gospels we find numerous references to fasting. It was viewed as a significant spiritual activity, and many of the Jewish religious leaders like the Pharisees fasted in order receive affirmation from others. Jesus spoke against this type of arrogant religious activity in his Sermon on the Mount. He said, "And when you fast, do not look gloomy like the hypocrites, for they disfigure their faces so that their fasting may be seen by others. I say to you, they have received their reward (Mt 6:16)." I'm hopeful that John the Baptist's followers practiced fasting with purer motives, yet Jesus was about to reveal that fasting was just a surface issue—they had a deeper, systemic problem.

Jesus' response was clear and concise. "Can the wedding guests mourn as long as the bridegroom is with them? The days will come when the bridegroom is taken

Day 5

away from them, and then they will fast (v. 15)." As you can see, Jesus gave a surface answer to their surface question. Basically, his answer was this: "My disciples don't need to fast because I'm here with them. I'm God's Son, the Messiah of Israel and the Bridegroom of the church. Like those at a wedding, they have great joy in my presence. When I return to heaven one day, they will mourn my absence, and they will fast."

    Jesus could have stopped his explanation there, but he didn't. He was ready to deal with the systemic problem now that the surface issue had been addressed. To do so he told two parables. First, Jesus told the parable of the torn garment. "No one puts a piece of unshrunk cloth on an old garment, for the patch tears away from the garment, and a worse tear is made (v.16)." Jesus said that you can't attach new material to old material that has already shrunk. If you do, when the new material shrinks it will tear away from the older material, which will only make the situation worse. Now if you don't sew, this parable may be confusing. Think about it another way. Have you ever tried to put a new nut on an old bolt? It never works. The old bolt may have corrosion or slight deformities. As a result, only the old nut will fit it. You have to put new nuts on new bolts for them to work correctly.

    Second, Jesus told the parable of the old wineskins. "Neither is new wine put into old wineskins. If it is, the skins burst and the wine is spilled and the skins are destroyed. But new wine is put into fresh wineskins, and so both are preserved (v. 17)." Jesus was making the same point in this parable. All wineskins lose their pliability with age. Since new wine expands in the fermenting process, it will burst old wineskins, and both the wine and the skin will be lost. Again, if you're not a winemaker this may seem strange. Several years ago I brought a machete home from Brazil. Today, both the blade and its scabbard are worn and seasoned

The goal of the new covenant is internal heart change, not external conformity to the law.

27

The Kingdom of God

> *The new covenant of Jesus' blood did not fix the Old Testament covenant of the law; it replaced it.*

with time and use. The old blade still returns with ease to its holder. Recently, I purchased a new machete with the intention of using my old scabbard. Forget about it. It simply won't fit. A new machete needs a new scabbard. Jesus' message was clear — you can't force new nuts onto old bolts, and you can't fill old scabbards with new swords.

Jesus told these parables, first, to reveal a truth about God's kingdom that neither the Pharisees nor the disciples of John had yet to understand: Jesus didn't come to earth to try and reform the old covenant between God and Israel. He came to institute a new covenant between God and the whole world, a covenant he would seal by the sacrifice of his life and the shedding of his blood (Heb 9:15-22). The gospel is the message of the new covenant—forgiveness is available to all on the basis of faith in the sacrificial death and victorious resurrection of Jesus Christ, God's Son.

This parable also reveals an important kingdom principle: The goal of the new covenant is internal heart change, not external conformity to the law. The Pharisees were all about external appearances (Mt 6:1-2a, 5), but Jesus was all about the heart (Mt 5:21- 48).

Remember yesterday's parable of the wheat and the weeds? Without revealed understanding of the gospel and saving faith in Jesus, humans seek their own justification according to their own standard. Like the Pharisees, many today seek to be justified, or made righteous, through external, religious activity. Trying to earn righteousness before God is like trying to fit new covenant nuts onto old covenant bolts. It leads only to exhaustion and despair.

> *God redeemed us to be transformed— to infuse us with character of Christ and a passion to pursue his mission.*

The principle of this parable also extends to those of us who

Day 5

have received the righteousness of Christ. While we live in our physical bodies, we daily battle our sin nature. It is easy for us to begin looking to our own spiritual activity for spiritual transformation. When we focus more on what we are doing *for* God, we open ourselves up to untruths that threaten our intimacy *with* God. We may begin to believe that God loves us because of what we do to serve Him. We may think that God owes us blessings because we have obeyed his commands. We may begin to bloat with pride at all we have accomplished. When we allow our hearts to fixate on spiritual activity, we cut ourselves off from the conviction and transformative power of the Holy Spirit within us.

When God forgives and redeems us, He gives us a new heart, a new identity, and a new future.

God redeemed us to transform us – to infuse us with the character of Christ and a passion to pursue his mission (Rom 12:1-2). The gospel is not a "quick fix" patch that we sew onto our beggars rags. It is not an engine fluid top-off kit. The new covenant of Jesus' blood did not fix the Old Testament covenant of the law; it replaced it. When God forgives and redeems us, He gives us a new heart, a new identity, and a new future.

The Kingdom of God

Food for Thought Have you ever paused to consider whether you view God only as a "quick fix"-- a source of help in a crisis or a means to appease others? Reflect on the rich truth of the gospel: that God did not save you to put a patch over your sin; he saved you to make you a brand new creation. Believer, pause to consider whether you are currently substituting spiritual activity for intimacy with God.

Faith in Action The fact that you are reading this book suggests that you desire an intimate relationship with God, your Father. Today, intentionally set and re-set your hope on Christ's performance on your behalf. You can serve him with joy, knowing that he has accomplished the work of salvation for you and that he will complete the work of transformation he has started in you (Phil. 1:6). "Jesus paid it all—all to him I owe. Sin had left a crimson stain—he washed it white as snow."

Prayer

When you pray today, talk with God about the condition of your heart. If you're substituting religious activity for spiritual transformation, confess it. If you're content with "quick fix" doses of God, confess that too. Ask God to grow you to spiritual maturity, so that your spiritual service will be motivated by love, grace, and the gospel.

Day 6

The Rich Man and Lazarus

Luke 16:19-31

I love movies that have great plot twists. That's the reason that I'm a fan of the Mission Impossible franchise. Along with the fact that these movies are packed with some of the best action stunts ever filmed, you never really know who is a good guy or a bad guy. Each movie is a literal roller-coaster of intrigue. There is one cool way that this mystery is maintained. The IMF team has the technology to create latex masks to copy anyone's face. And, through the use of vocal technology, they can simulate anyone's speech. In every movie, someone will be wearing a mask, but you never know who it is. It's always a shock when the person underneath is revealed.

Yesterday, we examined the futility of trying to earn our own righteousness, and we saw that religious activity cannot transform hearts. Today's parable addresses another common attempt to self-justify, and we will see that wealth cannot transform hearts.

In Luke 16, Jesus tells the fascinating story of two people, living two different kinds of lives, with two different spiritual trajectories. It's the only parable where Jesus named one of the characters, which has led some schol-

The Kingdom of God

> *You cannot be saved until you acknowledge that your only hope of salvation comes through faith in what Jesus did for you through his death and resurrection.*

ars to believe that it's not a parable at all, but an actual, historical account. That's what I believe – there was a literal man named Lazarus, who was gravely ill, and he was laid at the gate of a rich man's house in hopes of eating their trash. Regardless of whether this is an actual parable or not, it doesn't change the truth that this story contains about the kingdom of God.

Jesus did an amazing job describing the rich man. Obviously, he had lots of money. He lived in a compound, gated from the rest of the world. He wore beautiful clothes, and he ate sumptuous food every day. Everyone wanted to be like him. But as we will see, he was poor in what matters most in life.

Lazarus, on the other hand, had none of these material belongings. He had no money, home, beautiful clothing, or food. He was starving and very sick. Someone had cared enough about him to deposit him at the gate to the rich man's house. After all, the rich man was "religious." Surely, he would have mercy on Lazarus and help care for him. Yet, we read that the only relief for Lazarus came from the feral dogs that would stop to lick his sores and compete with him for the dinner scraps from the rich man's meals. Despite his circumstances, Lazarus was rich in what matters most in life. Notice what happens next.

"The poor man died and was carried by the angels to Abraham's side. The rich man died also and was buried (Lk 16:22)." We see, here, that death is no respecter of persons or power. Just as we have a birthday that is ordained by God, we each have a deathday that has been ordained by him as well. So it was for the rich man and Lazarus.

As Jesus continued the story, he revealed that death changes our position as it relates to the natural world, but it does not end our existence because our souls are im-

Day 6

mortal in the spiritual world (1 Cor 15). He continued, "In Hades, being in torment, he lifted up his eyes and saw Abraham far off and Lazarus at his side. And he called out, 'Father Abraham, have mercy on me, and send Lazarus to dip the end of his finger in water and cool my tongue, for I am in anguish in this flame (16:23-24).'" Can you imagine his surprise when the rich man realized that he was in hell? Can you imagine the surprise of the people listening to this story when they discovered that it was the rich man who was in hell?

In Jesus' day, many people thought that the way to determine someone's standing before God was to see how successful they were. But, the Bible doesn't say that having money means that you are blessed by God. Many unregenerate people have lots of money. Such was the case with the rich man. Yet, the Pharisees to whom Jesus was speaking, and nearly everyone else in that day, thought that money and success were what mattered most in this life, and they justified that mindset by attributing that success to God's blessing. Interestingly, the guy who went to hell in this story is the guy that everyone listening to Jesus likely wanted to be—rich and famous.

Jesus' disciples even struggled with this false assumption. Jesus told his disciples elsewhere, "Truly . . . only with difficulty will a rich person enter the kingdom of heaven. Again I tell you, it is easier for a camel to go through the eye of a needle than for a rich person to enter the kingdom of God (Mt 19:23- 24)." In ancient cultures, they shut the large city gates at night to protect against attacks from foreign armies or marauders. People still had to be able to get into the city at night, so they built small, one-person gates beside the large gates so that travelers could still enter at night. They called it the "eye of the needle." However, if you had a camel that you wanted to bring into the city after the big gates were closed, you were out of luck; most cam-

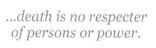

...*death is no respecter of persons or power.*

33

The Kingdom of God

els couldn't squeeze through that small opening. In other words, it's nearly impossible for a camel to fit through that small gate, but it's even more unlikely for a rich person to find the narrow gate that leads to life.

The disciples were shocked by this. They replied, "Who then can be saved (Mt 19:25)?" The disciples were convinced that rich people go to heaven also. After all, are they not blessed by God? By the world's standards, then, the rich man should go to heaven, and Lazarus should go to hell. After all, his illness proved that he was cursed by God, right? Wrong. In this parable, Jesus makes plain that neither financial standing nor health can indicate the status of one's heart.

Jesus continues the story by examining the rich man's reaction to being in hell. Not surprisingly, the rich man's first thought was about himself. He lived selfishly in life, and he remained the same in death. He said, "Father Abraham, have mercy on me, and send Lazarus to dip the end of his finger in water and cool my tongue, for I am in anguish in this flame (v. 24);" even in death he was bossing people around: "Hey Abraham, do what I say. Send Lazarus to serve me – that's his station. If he hadn't been so sick I might have hired him as one of my servants. Tell him to come take care of me." Can you imagine? Remember, the unregenerate will not be cured of evil in hell. Even in death, this selfish, self-righteous Pharisee was unchanged. He still wanted to be served by others.

Abraham replied, "Child, remember that you in your lifetime received your good things, and Lazarus in like manner bad things; but now he is comforted here, and you are in anguish. And besides all this, between us and you a great chasm has been fixed, in order that those who would pass from here to you may not be able, and none may cross from there to us (vv. 25-26)." Notice, those in paradise would have had the compassion to help the damned, but they were forbidden. Everyone in hell would escape immediately into paradise if given the chance, but they couldn't cross.

Day 6

Here, Jesus clarifies the importance of believing in and trusting in his saving work before death. When God opens our eyes (Eph 1:8) to the truth of the gospel, he gives us a chance to believe and to know, love, and serve him in this life; we won't get a second chance after we die.

Suddenly, the rich man remembered his family. The conversation went something like this. "Hey Abraham, it's me again. Apparently you're not going to help me—thanks for nothing! Anyway, I have another idea about how Lazarus can serve me. Tell him to leave the comfort of heaven, go back into that crummy world where nobody cared about him, and warn my brothers not to come here. They'll remember him—they used to walk by him at the gate every day. Tell Lazarus to warn them not to come to this place of torment (vv. 27-28, my paraphrase)."

Abraham must have rolled his eyes and sighed in amazement at the arrogance of this request. He replied, "Uh, no. Even if it were possible, which it isn't, I wouldn't send Lazarus back to warn your brothers. They can read Moses and the Prophets. Let them read the scriptures and listen to them (v. 29, my paraphrase)." The rich man's family could confirm Jesus' identity and deity in the scriptures (Lk 24:27). They could learn of the Messiah's descendance from David (Is 11) and birthplace in Bethlehem (Micah 5:2). They could read that he must suffer and die (Is 53) in the stead of sinners. They could anticipate the Messiah's eternal reign (Is 9:7).

Quickly, the rich man interrupted. "No, that's not good enough. NO, NO, NO. Father Abraham, you don't understand. If someone goes to them from the dead, they will repent. They don't want to listen to all that Old Testament stuff—it's all law anyway. It's so out of date, and parts of it really offend our modern sensibilities. But, if they talk with a dead guy that's come back to life, they will totally listen (v. 30, my paraphrase)!"

...*earthly status does not reflect one's status in the kingdom of God.*

The Kingdom of God

Quietly, and for the final time, Abraham responded to the rich man. "If they do not hear Moses and the Prophets, neither will they be convinced if someone should rise from the dead (v. 31)." Abraham reminded the rich man that God had already given his brothers the necessary truth to repent, believe, and experience a forever relationship with him. If they wouldn't believe the scriptures, it wouldn't matter if someone came back from the grave to warn them.

I cannot help but believe that Jesus was talking about himself as he ended this parable. Remember when he was hanging on the cross and the Pharisees were taunting him? "Come down off that cross and save yourself (Mk 15:30)." Jesus didn't come down from the cross. He had a mission to complete. However, it wouldn't have mattered if he had come down from the cross in a miraculous way – the religious leaders still would have rejected him.

They, too, had the Old Testament scriptures, yet they rejected him. They had been watching Jesus do miracles for more than three years, and they rejected him. After his resurrection, he appeared to hundreds of people (1 Cor 15:6). I'm sure some of them were these same Pharisees. Yet, rather than believe, they paid people to spread the lie that his body was stolen by his disciples. They didn't believe even when the Son of God came back from the dead.

In the parables, we see Jesus continue to draw a distinction between the external and the internal. Like the masks in the Mission Impossible franchise, appearances do not always match the condition of the heart. The story of the rich man and Lazarus strips the mask of wealth, revealing that earthly status does not reflect one's status in the kingdom of God. The rich man had all of the desires of his heart: family, money, house, possessions, respect. He didn't need anything from anyone. He had chosen to love money rather than God, and despite any religious activity, his heart was dark with unconfessed sin. Then he died, only to realize that self-sufficiency is an enemy of grace.

You cannot be saved until you acknowledge that your only hope of salvation comes through faith in what

Day 6

Jesus did for you through his death and resurrection. Neither religious activity nor wealth can rescue us or restore us to right standing before God. Our only hope for this life and the next is this: to be born again by faith in Jesus. When we trust in Christ's work of salvation on our behalf, God forgives our sin, fills and seals us with the Holy Spirit, adopts us into his spiritual family, gifts us to serve him through his Church, and promises us a forever with him. What an incredible gift!

The Kingdom of God

Food for Thought — Do you struggle to accept the truth that the people who reject God's offer of salvation will experience eternal torment, separated from God's gracious presence? In recent years, Christians have grown increasingly uncomfortable with the idea of a literal hell. False teachers cite God's nature in their arguments: God is Loving, Gracious, Merciful. Yes. He is also Just. He must right wrongs. Sin creates a debt that demands payment. Because of his nature, God could not ignore the death sentence earned by our sin. Instead, he took that sentence on himself, dying on the cross the death that each of us deserves. Jesus' death satisfied God's rightful and good wrath against evil and wickedness and all manner of injustice. Those who believe that Jesus' death was enough to pay their eternal sin debt are given receipts marked "Paid in Full." Take a moment to read Colossians 2:6-15.

Faith in Action — Reflect on the ways in which self-sufficiency is an enemy of grace. Are you relying on wealth, status, or religious activity to feel righteous? Ask God to reveal any self-sufficiency and to renew your dependence upon his grace for your confidence in his presence (Heb 4:14-16).

Prayer — Begin your prayer time today by thanking God for who he is: Gracious, Loving, Merciful, and Just. Thank him for paying your sin debt and welcoming you into his family. Then, talk with God about the tendency toward self-sufficiency. Confess as the Spirit convicts, and run again to the transforming grace of Jesus.

Day 7

Pharisee and the Tax Collector

Luke 18:9-14

One of the most famous state prisons in the US is Folsom Prison, located near Sacramento, CA. Made famous by the Johnny Cash song "Folsom Prison Blues," and by the concert he held there in 1968, Folsom Prison is an imposing granite structure that houses more than 2,000 male inmates.

Eight years after that famous concert, my Dad took me on a "field trip" to visit the prison since it was close to our home. Sounds crazy, right? My Dad was an F.B.I. agent, and he was committed to keeping me from ending up in a place like that. I'll never forget walking up to the large gate and waiting for it to swing slowly open. We traveled through a number of locked gates, each one closing behind us with a loud "clap." Finally, a guard led us into a long hallway toward one of the main prison wings. He stopped beside an iron door set on massive hinges embedded into the granite walls. Pulling a skeleton key from his keyring, he turned the lock and opened the door. Without a word, he pointed for me to go inside. I walked slowly into a 4' x 8' cell, containing an iron bed, a commode, and a sink. Suddenly, the door clanged shut behind me, and I heard the key turn in the lock. My Dad looked inside at me

The Kingdom of God

> *Daily calling to mind our need for gracious rescue keeps us running to God for daily grace.*

and said, "I want you to sit here for a while and consider what it would be like for this room to be your home for the next 10 years. I'll be back to get you in a while." With that, he turned and walked out of sight beside the guard.

For the next 30 minutes I sat in that cold, damp cell and listened to the sounds of the prison as they flowed through the granite. I could hear voices shouting in the distance, but the words were indistinct. The footfalls of the guards echoed down the hallway as they made their rounds; occasionally one walked by my cell without any acknowledgment. I felt the weight of loneliness settle down on me, and the thought of living in this horrid place filled my heart with dread. I don't think I was ever more grateful to see my Dad than when he reappeared with the guard to release me. We rode home in silence. We sat in the driveway before going into the house. Finally, my Dad spoke. "Son, there isn't a more horrific place on earth than prison. I never want to have to visit you there. Trust God, obey his word, and make wise choices. If you do this, you'll never deserve to end up in a place like that." With that, we got out of the car, and I never remember speaking about that trip with him again. We didn't have to—I had learned the lesson. Prison is terrifying.

Like me, you may have never spent a day of your life in prison. Or, perhaps you have, and you can still remember how difficult that experience was for you. Regardless, in today's parable, Jesus is going to communicate a shocking reality. In the spiritual world, we are each born into a spiritual prison called sin, and it makes us an enemy of God (Rom 6:20-21). Our status and judgment as sinners is actually declared by the scriptures. Paul wrote, "But the Scripture imprisoned everything under sin, so that the promise by faith in Jesus Christ might be given to those who believe (Gal 3:22)."

Day 7

In the foreword to the story, Luke tells us that Jesus told this parable about people who "trusted in themselves that they were righteous and treated others with contempt." In other words, they were prisoners to their own self-sufficiency. As we've examined for the last two days, those who have not understood and believed in the sufficiency of the death and resurrection of Jesus must look to substitutions for their righteousness—their right standing in the world. Today's parable describes two approaches to self-justification. Two spiritual prisons: religion and rebellion.

Jesus told about two men who chose to go to church. These two men couldn't be more different. One was a Pharisee, whom we know by now to be a self-proclaimed religious person. These men believed that a good Jew would obey both the written law given by Moses and the unwritten oral traditions of past teachers. The goal of the Pharisees was to help people avoid disobeying the 10 commandments. To this end, they codified no less than 613 additional laws that explained how to keep the 10 commandments in many different settings and situations. Over time, obeying the rules became more important than the purpose for obeying the rules—the system of the Pharisees became legalistic. Most Pharisees believed that they were righteous before God because of their work at keeping these laws.

The second man who went to church was a tax-collector. Few people in Israel were more despised than those who served in this role. The Romans would hire locals to collect the necessary taxes and tolls from the region. However, the Romans didn't pay their salaries. The tax collectors made money by overcharging the citizens and keeping the extra money for themselves (which they were allowed to do). As you might imagine, this could result in a lucrative business (cf. Zacchaeus, Lk 19). Yet, there was a tradeoff.

Only those who humbly admit and confess their sins experience God's forgiveness.

The Kingdom of God

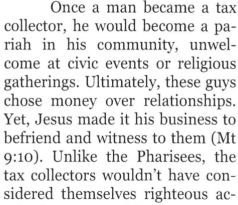

> We experience God's forgiveness through our humble confession of personal sin and our faith in Jesus Christ's sacrificial, atoning death and glorious resurrection.

Once a man became a tax collector, he would become a pariah in his community, unwelcome at civic events or religious gatherings. Ultimately, these guys chose money over relationships. Yet, Jesus made it his business to befriend and witness to them (Mt 9:10). Unlike the Pharisees, the tax collectors wouldn't have considered themselves righteous according to God's standard—they just wouldn't have cared because they sought justification according to a different standard than God's law: their own.

As the parable continued, Jesus gave us a glimpse into the worship of these two men: the Pharisee, who never missed church, and the tax collector, who never went to church. Jesus examined the Pharisee first. Like others in his group, he would have been standing in a place of prominence, praying where all could see and hear him (Mt 6:5). His prayer reveals much about his heart. "God, I thank you that I am not like other men, extortioners, unjust, adulterers, or even like this tax collector [imagine him pointing over at the tax collector who is being ridiculed in his prayer]. I fast twice a week; I give tithes of all that I get (v. 11-12)." Here, we see a man imprisoned by the sin of pride. He felt completely secure in his own self-righteousness and completely at ease in judging the life of the "wicked" tax collector. As a result, he couldn't see his own sin and need for a savior.

The prayer of the tax collector was different. He wasn't standing front and center like the Pharisee. Instead, he was standing "far off." It seems that he was in the temple, but just barely. Perhaps that was as far as any self-respecting Jew would allow him to go. Far from self-confident before God, he beat upon his chest with self-loathing. His prayer was simple and concise: "God, be merciful to me, a sinner (v. 13)." Here, we see a man whose sins are many and public. He extorted people for a living and used

Day 7

those gains for a lavish and self-indulgent lifestyle. Yet somehow, on this day, he had become painfully aware of his own sin and separation from God.

At face value, these men couldn't be more dissimilar. Yet, their lives are closer than you might think. First, both were trapped in the prison of sin—one was trapped by sinful religious pride, while the other was trapped by sinful personal greed. Second, both were in the right place—a building dedicated to the worship of God. Third, and finally, both were talking to the right person—the God who alone can provide forgiveness for their sins.

Here's something else to consider—our lives are closer to theirs than we'd like to admit. Whether we are religious or rebellious, until the gracious intervention of Jesus on our behalf, we are all trapped in a prison constructed by our own sins. The Bible says, "For all have sinned and fall short of the glory of God (Rom 3:23)." The penalty for these sins is physical and eternal death (Rom 6:23). That is the reason that God sent his only Son, Jesus, to die on the cross. When Jesus died, he paid the penalty that we each owe for our sin, so that we could be forgiven and restored to right relationship with God (1 Pet 3:18). Accepting God's offer of forgiveness requires us, first, to see our prison cell and, second, to cry out for rescue. So, what did the two men in the parable do? Jesus gave us the answer.

Speaking of the tax collector, he said, "I tell you, this man went down to his house justified, rather than the other [the Pharisee]. For everyone who exalts himself will be humbled, but the one who humbles himself will be exalted (v. 14)." This is how salvation works. Only those who humbly admit and confess their sins experience God's forgiveness. They are the ones who are "exalted" through eternal adoption into God's spiritual family. Those pride-filled people who trust in their own self-righteousness will be "humbled" through eternal separation from God in hell. Jesus' kingdom principle in this parable is clear: We experience God's forgiveness through our humble confession of personal sin and our faith in Jesus Christ's sacrificial, atoning death and glorious resurrection. As we walk with

The Kingdom of God

Christ, we must intentionally remember who we were without Christ—a locked up prisoner. We must remember our inability to open the iron door of that cell. Daily calling to mind our need for gracious rescue keeps us running to God for daily grace. Remembering leads to continued confession of sin and a closer walk with Jesus.

Day 7

Food for Thought The Pharisee and the Tax Collector in this parable represent every person who does not know Jesus. They are the religious lost, who are trusting in their good works to save them, or the secular lost, who seek to justify themselves apart from God's standard. Neither the religious nor the secular lost has understood the gospel. Both are trapped in a spiritual prison. Both need Christ. Pause to consider who you were before the grace of God reached you in Christ. Thank him for saving you. Then, consider how your sin nature flares up – in self-righteousness and judgment of others, or in rebellion against God's laws? Ask for the grace to follow Jesus faithfully today.

Faith in Action Take some time to reflect on how to share the hope of Christ with these two categories of people. Pharisees must become convinced that they cannot be saved by their works (Eph 2:8-9; Gal 2:16; Mt 7:21-23). Tax Collectors, on the other hand, must become convinced that there is a God to whom they will give an account for their lives (Heb 4:13; 2 Chron 16:9). Identify a few people you know in each category.

Prayer

In your prayer time today, remember to pray for your family and friends who are represented by the Pharisee and Tax Collector in today's parable. Pray for them by name. Ask God to enlighten them to the truth of the gospel through the Holy Spirit. Ask God to give you the opportunity for gospel conversations with them.

Day 8

The Great Banquet

Luke 14:12-24

Years ago my wife and I had the privilege to visit Germany. While we were there, we visited a couple of old castles that are still intact. Each one had a meeting hall. They were large, impressive structures, with wood-beamed ceilings and walls adorned with beautiful tapestries and imposing fireplaces. I tried to imagine what it would have been like to attend an event there centuries ago. I pictured the wealthy of the community gathering for great feasts and celebrations. Perhaps, on certain occasions, the whole community would be invited to attend. The household staff would work for days to move the furniture, roll up the carpet, prepare the meal, and ready the guest rooms. The invited guests would receive a hand-crafted invitation. They would spend time preparing an appropriate outfit and planning their route to arrive on time. Finally, they would step inside the grand room, walls ablaze with candles and tables lined with food. These halls held celebrations I would not have wanted to miss!

In today's parable, Jesus is at such a banquet. While the text does not note the size of this particular banquet, we do know that it is being hosted by a "ruler of the Pharisees (Lk 14:1)." That means that he held a significant place of honor in the culture, and his parties would have looked far different from other parties Jesus occasionally attend-

The Kingdom of God

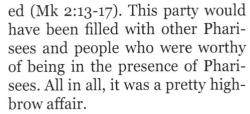

...God's house will be filled with people from every tribe, tongue, kindred, and nation, and we will dwell together with him for eternity.

ed (Mk 2:13-17). This party would have been filled with other Pharisees and people who were worthy of being in the presence of Pharisees. All in all, it was a pretty highbrow affair.

Imagine sitting around that great table with Jesus and the "who's who" of society. Perhaps you are elated to have been invited; perhaps you expected to be invited because of your clout. Either way, it's about to get really awkward for everyone at the table.

Jesus waited for a quiet moment and then addressed his host. "Hey, the next time you host a banquet, don't invite all of your family, friends, and rich neighbors. When you do that, you're always guaranteed a return invite. Instead, invite the poor, the crippled, the lame, and the blind. They can't repay you, so you'll be assured a reward at the final resurrection (vv. 12-14, my translation)." When he was done, the silence was deafening. In one simple statement, Jesus upended the entire process of hosting and attending parties in his day, especially parties that were being hosted by "religious" people. The moment became so awkward, that one of the guests broke the silence: "Blessed is everyone who will eat bread in the kingdom of God (v. 15)." In essence, this guest went straight for the Sunday School answer: "Amen, brother, heaven's going to be great!" Rather than wrestle with the truth of Jesus' statement, he finds a comment everyone can agree on. After all, stating general platitudes is far easier than attempting life-change.

Jesus probably stared at the guy who made this ridiculous statement for a few moments before responding. Then, he told today's parable to the assembled guests. He began, "A man once gave a great banquet and invited many. And at the time for the banquet he sent his servant to say to those who had been invited, 'Come, for everything is now ready (vv. 16-17).'"

Day 8

Here, we see the ancient banquet system described. A wealthy man, who could afford a banquet hall in his home, would send out invitations to his intended guests. He would have invited friends, wealthy clients, select politicians, and fellow aristocrats. These folks were invited with an understanding that reciprocity was in order. He never would have invited his acquaintances, complete strangers, or his enemies. The invitations themselves were unique, too. They would go out first in written form, but on the day of the event, his servants would go and personally announce that the banquet feast was ready. This served as a form of reminder about the party – like an ancient Google Calendar notification. Then, the invited guests would make their way to the banquet. Jesus described the banquet in this parable as a "great banquet." The word he used means "mega." It was clearly going to be an amazing party! You can imagine how excited the guests would be to attend. Or, would they?

As the servants made their rounds, they noticed that something was terribly wrong. One by one, the invited guests began to make excuses, declining the invitation. The first guest said that he had purchased property and needed to go inspect it (v. 18). The second guest said that he had purchased 10 oxen and needed to go inspect them (v. 19). The third guest said that he had recently been married, so he needed to be excused (v. 20). On and on the excuses poured in – none of the invited guests planned to attend the great banquet. Slowly, the servants returned to their master and reported the sad news.

As you might imagine, the master of the house became angry. Consider how he must have felt. What if you had gone to great expense of time and money planning a big event at your house for your friends, and on the day of the event they all texted you with an excuse for not attending. Would that upset you? It sure would upset me, and it upset the

Everyone receives an invitation to the banquet, but only the spiritually poor will accept and attend.

49

The Kingdom of God

master in Jesus' parable, too. He had a banquet hall full of amazing food and beverages, but he had no one present to enjoy it. That's when he did the most unusual and unexpected thing. He gave his servants a different task: "Go out quickly to the streets and lanes of the city, and bring in the poor and crippled and blind and lame (v. 21)." Sometime later his servants returned. They had done as he asked, but there was still plenty of room in the banquet hall. So, the master sent them back out. "Go out to the highways and hedges and compel people to come in, that my house may be filled (v. 23)."

    The master told his servants to "compel" the people to come to the feast. Sometimes this word means to "force" someone to do something. But in this context, the word means to use "earnest persuasion" to convince them to do something. While it may seem strange that anyone would need compelling to attend a feast, think about it in this way. The people the master was now inviting had never been to a fine house like his; they had never eaten fine food like his; they had never had fine wine like his. I'm sure some of them thought it was a trick. "What? Go up to that big house in town? Join the rich guy for a feast? Someone like me? I'm not falling for that! He would never invite the likes of me to his house!" Yet, the servants worked as hard as they could to persuade them to attend, and attend they did.

    Like my own amazement at the meeting halls in German castles, I imagine the people in Jesus' parable felt overwhelmed. Though they could not give him anything in return, the host had extended a generous invitation toward them. What gratitude and joy must they have felt and expressed to the banquet's host.

    If you remember, Jesus began this teaching moment by telling the host of his banquet not to invite the people who could repay him. Instead, he should invite the poor, weak, and marginalized in his community to a banquet. This would lead to reward at the resurrection of the just. Jesus could have stopped his parable here to convey

Day 8

a resounding practical message with his listeners: love and serve those who cannot repay you.

Yet, as he concluded the parable, Jesus gives the story an eschatological twist, looking to the literal end of the age and God's great banquet: "For I tell you, none of those men who were invited shall taste my banquet (v. 24)." For I tell you. What began as a metaphorical story suddenly became a reality. Everyone at the table would have been shocked when they heard Jesus' claim.

Clearly, Jesus was speaking about the kingdom of God. From this parable, we learn two key truths about God's kingdom. The first is this: everyone receives an invitation to the banquet, but only the spiritually poor will accept and attend.

In the parable, Jesus draws a distinction between the expected and the unexpected guests. The expected guests – the wealthy, healthy, and well-known – accept the initial invitation but make excuses when it is time to attend the banquet. As we saw over the last two days of our study, self-sufficiency, which is often bolstered by wealth and physical health, is an enemy of grace. Like the Pharisees, many religious people in our day are content and confident in their own good works. They hear the story about forgiveness by grace alone through faith in the death and resurrection of Jesus, but they reject it. The non-religious similarly dismiss the good news about Jesus, but their brand of self-sufficiency trusts their own knowledge of the natural world or their own ability to create happiness. Regardless of what they are trusting in to be fed, in the last days, Jesus makes clear that they will not taste his banquet.

The unexpected guests who attend the banquet in the parable are the blind, the lame, the crippled, the poor, and the marginalized. In God's kingdom, those who accept the invitation and attend his banquet with joy and awe are those who recognize their utter spiritual poverty and desperate need for mercy. They see the invitation to God's banquet for what it is – undeserved, unmerited favor. In

The Kingdom of God

the last days, they will feast together with Jesus at the wedding supper of the Lamb (Rev 19:6-9).

The second kingdom principle we learn through this parable is this: God's house will be filled. The fact that earth remains and that our days are prolonged proves that there is still room in the banquet hall (2 Pet 3:8-10). While we wait for the return of Jesus and the initiation of his banquet, let us pray for and compel those around us to accept their invitation. Then, let us live with joy knowing that God's house will be filled with people from every tribe, tongue, kindred, and nation, (Rev 5:9) and we will dwell together with him for eternity.

Day 8

Food for Thought

Read 2 Peter 3:1-13 and reflect on the reasons why Jesus has not yet returned. Call to mind the specific people God has placed in your life who have not yet repented and trusted Christ, and pray for the continued patience of God on their behalf.

Faith in Action

In addition to truths about the nature of God's kingdom, parables often contain practical implications. When was the last time that you hosted a dinner and invited your lost neighbors, co-workers, or friends? Sharing around the table is one of the best ways to live out your faith, even if all they see is your saying a blessing of grace over the meal. Consider also what it would look like to host a party where you invited only those who couldn't repay you. Think about ways that you can bless the less fortunate. If you do, you will be repaid at the resurrection of the just.

Prayer

In your prayer time today, talk with God about the status of your witness. How are you doing in your living out and sharing of the gospel? Pray for the lost people in your world. Ask God to give you a chance to share the gospel with them. Then, ask God to show you ways to model his grace through your generosity to them, especially those who can't repay you.

Day 9

The Narrow Door

Luke 13:22-30

In 1999, my wife Lyla and I were in England conducting research for my dissertation. I was studying the life and preaching ministry of an English evangelist named Rodney "Gypsy" Smith (cf. Gypsy Smith: The Forgotten Evangelist). We spent two weeks in musty basements around cramped library carousels collecting information. On our final day in England, we went sightseeing in London. When we paused in front of Buckingham Palace, we noticed that the flag was flying that day which meant that the Queen was present. She was inside the palace, just a few hundred feet from us. I could see her guards standing watch. But I left without entering the palace grounds or meeting the Queen. Though I was proximally close to the Queen that day, I could not claim to be close to her relationally.

In today's text, Jesus is speaking to an audience similar to other listeners we have encountered so far in our study of the parables. They often looked to external factors like proximity, power, or position to discern someone's righteousness, or standing, before God. They believed that because they had spent some time around Jesus that they actually knew Jesus. Or, that since they spent time doing activity for God, they had a relationship with God. In his teaching today, Jesus continues the systematic unravel-

Kingdom Residents

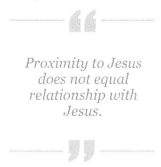

Proximity to Jesus does not equal relationship with Jesus.

ing of his audience's assumptions about God's kingdom.

Luke tells us that Jesus was traveling through "towns and villages" teaching the message of the kingdom. On one of his teaching stops, a listener asked, "Lord, will those who are saved be few?" This is a great question. After all, if you hear about God's kingdom, wouldn't you want to know how to become a part of it?

Jesus' answer reveals significant truths about Kingdom residency. First, he describes the entrance to God's kingdom. He said, "Strive to enter through the narrow door. For many, I tell you, will seek to enter and will not be able (v. 24)." The words "narrow door" depict an entrance that cannot admit many people at once. Can you visualize the broad entrances of theme parks like Disney World? Large, well-marked entrances permit large crowds to find, enter, and exit the gates without much difficulty. Jesus paints the opposite picture of the entrance to God's kingdom. The door is narrow.

When I read this verse in Luke, I always think of some similar verses in Matthew 7:13-14, in which Jesus enhances our understanding of Kingdom entrance. He said, "Enter by the narrow gate. For the gate is wide and the way is easy that leads to destruction, and those who enter by it are many. For the gate is narrow and the way is hard that leads to life, and those who find it are few." He adds to our vision of the narrow door a picture of the wide gate and the roads beyond each entrance.

The wide gate is easy to find. In fact, since the moment sin entered the world, the wide road has been the default position for every person. It is also easy to follow. No one needs help navigating this road; self-sufficiency thrives on the wide road since our own intellect and strength suffice to keep us directed toward the destination. We crave what we believe to be the ends of our strivings on the wide road: power, pleasure, possessions or merely the

Day 9

independence and freedom to make our own decisions. On the wide road, we believe that we do not even need a guide, let alone a savior. It is easy. We can do it by ourselves.

By comparison, the narrow gate and road is both hard to find and to follow. The door to God's kingdom is hard to find because it opens only through acknowledgment of need. While self-sufficient religious activity can give the appearance of belonging to God's kingdom, Jesus teaches that the kingdom belongs to those who see their need for mercy and look not to their own merits or efforts but to Jesus for rescue. In fact, in John 10, Jesus calls himself "the door (v. 9)."

He describes a sheepfold with a gate through which sheep exit to find pasture in the day and enter to rest in the night. He said, "I am the door. If anyone enters by me, he will be saved and will go in and out and find pasture (v. 9)."

Access to God's kingdom can only be gained through the saving work of Jesus. Once we recognize that we cannot save ourselves, and we place our faith in the finished work of Jesus on our behalf, we gain access to the narrow road. Our location shifts from "wide road" to "narrow road," and with it our residency. Through the narrow door of Christ, we belong to God's kingdom.

We will see in the days ahead that the narrow road is not just hard to find but also hard to follow. It is costly. Unlike the wide road, navigating the narrow road requires total denial of self-sufficiency, for our entrance was gained through the sacrifice of Another and our membership is sustained through the power of Another. We are utterly dependent on the grace of God for the totality of our Kingdom journey: our entrance through the narrow gate, our navigation of the costly road, and our arrival to eternity.

We are utterly dependent on the grace of God for the totality of our Kingdom journey: our entrance through the narrow gate, our navigation of the costly road, and our arrival to eternity.

In both teachings on the wide and narrow doors, Jesus gave

Kingdom Residents

> With the assurance of eternal life, not even death itself can threaten the abundant life of a Kingdom resident.

insight into the destination of each road. Of the wide road, Jesus said it "leads to destruction (Mt 7:13)." We understand "destruction" to mean eternal separation from God in hell, the place of punishment for those who reject God's offer of Kingdom residency. Luke 13 tells us that while the offer of salvation is available now, it will not always remain so. Jesus said, "When once the master of the house has risen and shut the door, and you begin to stand outside and to knock at the door, saying 'Lord, open to us.' Then he will answer you, 'I do not know where you come from (v. 25).'" In other words, there comes a time in everyone's life when God closes the narrow door. That is why the Bible says that today is the day of salvation (2 Cor 6:2). We are never promised tomorrow. If we're to enter God's kingdom through the narrow door, we must do so while we have the opportunity.

When Jesus finished speaking, the objections began immediately. Not be able to enter? "We ate and drank in your presence, and you taught in our streets (v. 26)." I can hear them arguing their case before God on the Day of Judgment. "We spent some time with you. You came to our town. You walked on our streets. I mean, we even ate in the same restaurant one time. How can it be that you're not going to let us into your eternal kingdom?" God's response will be simple, clear, and damning, "'I tell you, I do not know where you come from. Depart from me, all you workers of evil (vv. 27-28)!'"

Considering what we have studied about many of Jesus' listeners, we can understand their confusion. They believed the kingdom belonged to the rich, the healthy, and the outwardly religious. Those who spent the most time in the temple, prayed the loudest prayers, invited Jesus to their banquets – surely they would be counted among the residents of God's kingdom. They had bought into the fallacy of proximity. Instead, Jesus informed his

Day 9

hearers that many will seek to enter – perhaps even feel entitled to enter – but will be unable because proximity to Jesus does not equal relationship with Jesus.

Perhaps you know someone who thinks about their faith in terms of proximity. They believe that they're going to be fine when they die because they hung out with Jesus a few times. Maybe they went to church occasionally, put a few dollars in the plate, and tried to be a good person. Yet Jesus said these explanations wouldn't be enough to get into heaven (Mt 7:21-23) because proximity to the door does not equal entrance through the door.

In reality, they were like me on my visit to Buckingham Palace. They walked up to the fence occasionally and peered at God's kingdom. Yes, Jesus was in there somewhere, but they never met him. They never walked inside; they simply chose to hang out occasionally by the gate. When they die, they will spend eternity separated from God. "For the gate is wide and the way is easy that leads to destruction, and those who enter by it are many (Mt 7:13)."

Mercifully, Jesus did not end his teaching here. He also gave a glimpse of the narrow road's destination: "For the gate is narrow and the way is hard that leads to life (Mt 7:14)." While the narrow road is costly and can invite temporal suffering, it leads to life that is truly life. Jesus himself said that he came to be the door to God's kingdom so that we may have "life and have it abundantly (Jn 10:10)." We can experience abundant life in any circumstance when we are in Christ because we know our destination. In Luke 13, Jesus included a final image of our eternal future. He described Abraham, Isaac, Jacob, the prophets, and saints "from east and west, and from north and south [reclining] at table in God's kingdom (v. 29)." Residency in God's kingdom promises a future of rest, dwelling in security with God and brothers and sisters in Christ forever. With the assurance of *eternal* life, not even death itself can threaten the abundant life of a Kingdom resident.

Kingdom Residents

Food for Thought — It has always been unpopular to suggest that one can only gain entrance to God's kingdom through the narrow door. The "one summit, many trails" narrative continues to gain support in a society whose only mandate is to "live your truth." Read John 10:1-18, and consider what Jesus has to say about the pathway to relationship with God and residency in his kingdom. For further reflection, read John 14:6 and John 15:1-11. Rehearse the truth of the gospel, both for your own encouragement and for the readiness to share the hope that you have in Christ with others today.

Faith in Action — Would you characterize the life you are living as "abundant"? Like Jesus' audience, we can be tempted to view our quality of life through the external lenses of our possessions, health, or comfort, but Jesus came to give us life "to the full (Jn 10:10, NIV)." Turn your eyes upon Jesus throughout your day, and allow the lens of eternity to shape your perception of your circumstances. "Through death into life everlasting he passed and we follow him there. O'er us sin no more hath dominion, for more than conquerors we are!"

Prayer — Spend time praising God for the privilege of being a Kingdom resident. Express gratitude to God for allowing you to enter the narrow door by faith in his son Jesus. Then, confess any shortsightedness that limits your belief in the abundant life Jesus has given to you in the here and now. Ask for eyes to see your circumstances through the lens of all you have in Christ and all you are promised in eternity. God has been faithful to grant us faith, and He will sustain our faith until the end. Thanks be to him!

Day 10

Hidden Treasure

Matthew 13:44-46

When I was a boy, I received an illustrated copy of Robert Louis Stevenson's Treasure Island. I was mesmerized as I read about young Jim Hawkins' daring adventures with the pirate Long John Silver. From that day to this, I have loved stories about the pursuit of buried treasure.

Even in Jesus' day people knew all about the reality of buried treasure. So, they probably weren't surprised when Jesus used the subject in two of his parables. In the first, Jesus described a man who found some treasure when he wasn't even looking for it (v. 44). That wasn't an unusual occurrence in Jesus' day. People didn't have the luxury of using banks like we do. As a result, they would often hide their assets in the ground, or a wall in their house, or even a wall around their home for fear of thieves or enemy invasion. Others would carry their treasure with them. If they were in danger of being overrun by marauders, they would hide their treasure wherever they were, hoping to recover it when the threat had passed.

Hiding their resources would offer some protection, but occasionally, owners would die without telling anyone the location of their treasures. Often, their treasures would remain hidden for years only to be discovered later by others.

Because this was such a common occurrence, the Jews had developed numerous laws to help determine what

Kingdom Residents

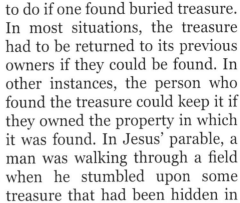

> Residence in God's kingdom is costly and priceless. It is of immeasurable worth, and possessing it reorders one's whole life.

to do if one found buried treasure. In most situations, the treasure had to be returned to its previous owners if they could be found. In other instances, the person who found the treasure could keep it if they owned the property in which it was found. In Jesus' parable, a man was walking through a field when he stumbled upon some treasure that had been hidden in the field long ago. Perhaps erosion had unearthed it and the golden coins were simply laying on the surface, gleaming in the sun. He must have stooped to examine his find, his curiosity turning to joy. He quickly covered the treasure with dirt and rocks so that no one else would find it. Then, he went and sold all of his property so that he could buy the field and the immense treasure it contained.

In today's second parable, Jesus told a story about someone who was a treasure hunter by trade (vv. 45-46). It was his business to buy and sell pearls. We don't think of pearls very often when we're thinking about costly gems. But in ancient Rome, pearls were highly valued and sought after by the wealthy. Often, they were used as capital for purchases. When Jesus talked about a pearl merchant in search of gems, his listeners would have been familiar with their value and worth. In this parable, the merchant discovers the most amazing pearl he has ever seen. It's perfect in size, form, and color. He knows that it's worth a lot of money. As a result, he leaves to sell all that he possesses, and he returns with all of his money and buys it. Jesus used these two examples to further our understanding of God's kingdom. Here, he tells us that God's kingdom is both costly and priceless. It is of immeasurable worth, and possessing it reorders one's whole life.

Jesus knew that every person in the world is looking for the same treasure—they're just looking in the wrong places. In Ecclesiastes 3:11, Solomon wrote that God "has

Day 10

put eternity into man's heart." Because everyone is made in God's image, we're all looking for treasure that only God can supply. In modern society, this treasure can be reduced to three basic needs. First, everyone is looking for a sense of personal significance; we all want to be loved and valued. We want to know that we matter, and that we matter to someone. Second, everyone is looking for personal success; we all want to achieve some level of success and be appreciated for our contributions. Third, everyone is looking for personal pleasure; we all want to be happy and fulfilled in our lives.

As we saw yesterday, the wide road promises to satisfy our need for personal significance, success, and pleasure. It offers the freedom to chart our own course; we can be master of our fate. We need answer to no one. But it is all an illusion because the wide road leads to disappointment and destruction. Only God can satisfy all of the desires of our hearts. In Christ, he offers us unconditional love and the assurance of our value in his sight. He demonstrated just how much he loves and values us by sending his only Son into the world to defeat our sin, conquer the grave, and make a way for us to be in relationship with him (Eph 2:1-10). He created us for an eternal purpose, and laid out good works for us to do (Eph 2:10). He provides fulfilling joy through our living hope, Jesus Christ. He is the treasure, and through him, we are born again to "an inheritance that is imperishable, undefiled, and unfading (1 Pet 1:4)." The treasure God offers in Christ will never lose its value.

The treasure finders in today's parables were faced with an "all or nothing" situation: pursue the treasure they had found or abandon it. In obtaining the precious pearl and the buried treasure, they gave up everything they possessed. They attached all of their significance, security, and hopes for future success to the treasure they found.

The treasure God offers in Christ will never lose its value.

Kingdom Residents

> When we forsake earthly treasures to follow Jesus, our lives bear witness to the immeasurable worth of the treasure of Christ.

God's kingdom is like that. Residency is an "all or nothing" identity. It is impossible to possess dual citizenship on the wide and narrow road. Entrance through the narrow door of faith in Jesus seals our residency in God's kingdom. As a result, we can live with great assurance that we belong to Christ. Yet, like the buried treasure and the pearl, residency is costly. Following Christ necessitates forsaking earthly treasures. When we forsake earthly treasures to follow Jesus, our lives bear witness to the immeasurable worth of the treasure of Christ.

Throughout his ministry, Jesus identified three markers of Kingdom residency. First, Kingdom residents submit to the lordship of King Jesus. In Luke 9:23-25, Jesus said, "If anyone would come after me, let him deny himself and take up his cross daily and follow me... For what does it profit a man if he gains the whole world and loses or forfeits himself?" Submission to the lordship of Jesus is a willingness to abandon my own life plans in favor of embracing the plans that God has for me, even if those plans lead to a cross. This is the only way to follow Jesus. Unbelievers who reject the lordship of Christ in pursuit of their own interests may gain the whole world, but they will spend eternity in hell (Mk 8:36).

Second, residency in God's kingdom is marked by servanthood. Many times, Jesus found his disciples discussing their individual gifts and contributions to God's kingdom. In fact, hours before his arrest, they were trying to figure out who was the greatest (Lk 22:24-27). When Jesus heard them, he reminded them that greatness in God's kingdom isn't measured by ability; it's measured by service. He said, "I am among you as one who serves (v.27)." Following Christ is marked by a servant's heart.

Third, residency in God's kingdom is marked by sacrifice. In Luke 9:57-63, Jesus is approached by three

Day 10

different people who expressed a desire to follow him. Jesus, knowing their hearts, exposed each person's barrier to following him sacrificially. The first may have loved comfort and stability, for when he told Jesus he would follow him anywhere, Jesus said to him, "Foxes have holes, and birds of the air have nests, but the Son of Man has nowhere to lay his head." The second may have hoarded the resource of time, for his excuse seems logical to us – "Let me first go and bury my father." But Jesus saw the deeper heart issue and said to him, "Leave the dead to bury their own dead. But as for you, go and proclaim the kingdom of God." The third may have feared the unknown, for he said "I will follow you, Lord, but let me first say farewell to those at my home." Perhaps he questioned whether following Jesus was really worth leaving his home, family, and career pursuits. To him, Jesus said, "No one who puts his hand to the plow and looks back is fit for the kingdom of God."

Those conversations remind me of a similar story found in Mark 10. When the rich young ruler came to Jesus, he was ready to follow, as long as he could do so on his own terms. Jesus again cut right to the heart of his particular barrier to faith: "Go, sell all that you have and give to the poor, and you will have treasure in heaven; and come, follow me (v.21)." The young man left with a sad heart. He chose his financial security over surrender and sacrifice. Each of these would-be followers liked the idea of following Jesus, and they probably enjoyed their proximity to Jesus. However, when confronted with the costs of following Jesus, their excuses revealed an unwillingness to sacrifice their time, resources, or relationships. Sadly, they failed to understand the value gained in return for their surrender. In today's parables, the finders of the buried treasure and the pearl, having recognized the true worth of their discoveries, gladly gave up all they had previously possessed. Sacrificing lesser joys is easy in the face of priceless treasure.

Kingdom Residents

Food for Thought All around the world, people who follow Jesus face real-world consequences. They can lose their jobs, their families, and their lives. Every time they meet for worship they risk imprisonment. Read 1 Peter 1:3-9, and spend some time today reflecting on the worth of life in Christ and your own willingness to undergo risk to follow Jesus. Consider, these questions: If I could lose my job, my family, or my life because I'm a Christian, would I still live as a worshiper? If I risked arrest today because I'm a Christian, would I still follow Christ?

Faith in Action Today, look for ways to give evidence to those around you that you are a resident in God's kingdom. Think about how to display the greatness of the treasure that you possess in Christ so that others will see it and desire it. One of the great ways to do this is through the use of faith language. When you really know Jesus, it can't help but show up in your speech. For instance, when talking about your plans, including the phrase "Lord willing" demonstrates an understanding of God's sovereignty and our lack of control. When talking about a big decision in your life, referencing prayer shows a dependence on God's guidance and trust in his will: "My wife and I are praying about whether to buy a house." Finally, offering to pray for people when they share a problem from their lives reveals your faith in God's power: "I'm sorry to hear that. Can I pray for you today about that situation?" Using faith language gives you a way to reveal that you're a person of faith, and it may open the door for future conversations about the gospel.

Prayer

Spend some time today praying for your fellow Christians who live in dangerous places around the world. Ask God to protect and preserve them. Ask God to use their lives and witness to point others towards Jesus! To help with this, search for the song "I Will Stand" by Broken Lantern Project on YouTube. Let the significance of persecution in the world keep you prayerful for the persecuted church.

Day 11

Tower/Army

Luke 14:25-33

It is difficult to hear criticism, let alone receive it. While we're all experts at receiving praise, receiving a word of rebuke stings our ego every time. We can all remember a time when a parent, coach, or boss had to get onto us about something in our life. Can you remember any of those times? Years ago I served with a dear friend at a church plant in Atlanta. We were experiencing tremendous growth and the demands of the ministry were great. It was my first real ministry experience, and I was way over my head in some areas. I remember my friend sitting me down and challenging me about my need to speed up my learning curve so that I could become more effective. I'll have to tell you—that is still one of the hardest conversations I've ever had to endure. At first, I found lots of reasons to be upset about it. But in the end, that conversation became a catalyst for some of the best growth in my life.

In today's parable, Jesus is going to say some of his most challenging words to the people who were following him. Luke 14:25 tells us that "great crowds accompanied him," which should give us pause after hearing Jesus' description of the narrow door to the kingdom of God. Jesus understood that many in the crowd were following him with a faulty understanding of Kingdom residency. They followed Jesus for what he could provide for them in

Kingdom Residents

> *Renouncing all is denying the world's attempts to provide significance, comfort, and hope for the future.*

the here and now – maybe healing, loaves and fish, or a front-row seat to his anticipated rise to political stardom. They had yet to understand the true cost – and the true value -- of following Jesus. Knowing the hearts of the crowd, Jesus stopped for an impromptu teaching moment.

He said, "If anyone comes to me and does not hate his own father and mother and wife and children and brothers and sisters, yes, and even his own life, he cannot be my disciple (v. 26)." This statement could be the original "come to Jesus" meeting. Jesus doesn't admonish the crowds to love God a little more than their families or to rearrange their priorities. He says, instead, if you do not hate your family and your own life, you *cannot be my disciple.*

We rightly read this statement as a rebuke of their external motives for following Jesus. They obviously misunderstood the purpose of discipleship and the costs it entailed. But, our sensibilities may balk at the word "hate." After all, God created marriage and family, and they play a significant role in his will for our lives. Yet, in his continued effort to explain the glory of life in God's kingdom, Jesus again flips earthly expectations. Family, what we often hold up as the highest good on earth, Jesus tells us to hate. Our very lives, what we often seek to preserve with all of our resources, Jesus tells us to hate.

In doing so, Jesus is not advocating for the poor treatment of our loved ones or for self-harm; he is emphasizing both the value and the cost of discipleship. That physical family, which we often hold up as the highest good on earth, cannot compare to the joy of being in the family of God; therefore, we must orient our lives toward the kingdom first, forsaking all others. Doing so will look different in each family. For many believers around the world today, following Jesus means literally forsaking their earthly families because their earthly families will

Day 11

forsake them if they claim Christ. Others must sacrifice their family's expectations, plans, and priorities for their lives in order to follow Jesus' commands, surrender to Jesus' control, and pursue Jesus' priorities for their lives. Jesus speaks into each situation: Yes, even so, follow me – I am worth the cost.

In the same way, that physical life which we often seek to preserve with all of our resources is rendered utterly unprofitable (Mk 8:36) in light of the riches of the abundant life found in Christ; therefore, we must surrender our desire for personal safety and commit to follow Jesus even unto death. Jesus said, "Whoever does not bear his own cross and come after me *cannot be my disciple* (v. 27, emphasis mine)." The import of these words is often lost on us in the 21st century. Today, crosses are worn as jewelry. But in Jesus' day, the word "cross" was death language. All of his followers had seen the horror of crucifixion. Yet, Jesus called his disciples to follow him regardless of the cost to personal safety. Ultimately, our understanding of the value of following Jesus enables us to endure the cost of following Jesus and to surrender the blessings of life and family to his will.

Jesus then told two parables to help us understand his message. The first parable asked the audience to think about a man who wanted to build a vineyard tower. The audience would have been familiar with these structures, as they were commonly built for several purposes: they helped the managers oversee the vineyard workers, provided protection from the weather or thieves, and served as the resting place for the guards at night. Jesus asked, "which of you, desiring to build a tower, does not first sit down and count the cost, whether he has enough to complete it? (v. 28)." Wisdom says not to start a building project if you don't have enough money to finish. Jesus said that failing to count the cost would lead to ridicule: "Otherwise, when

We must value God more than anything else in our lives.

he has laid a foundation and is not able to finish, all who see it begin to mock him, saying, 'This man began to build and was not able to finish (v. 29).'" In this situation, the builder had the capacity to calculate the cost of the materials and labor and to make an informed decision whether to begin construction. Not doing so would be absurd; he would not only risk ridicule but also face the possibility of investing all of his resources in a half-built tower incapable of fulfilling any of its intended purposes.

The second parable was about a king who discovers that his kingdom will soon be under attack. In Jesus' day, if a king lost a war, it could have devastating effects upon both the people and him. A conquered king would often be blinded, have his hands and feet cut off, and then be placed upon a stake until gravity and physiology caused him to be impaled and die. The conquering king would often take his wives and children, and subjugate his kingdom. Clearly, this was a fate that every king tried to avoid. As a result, when the enemy was still a long way off, the king would begin to count the cost. Jesus said that the king in this parable was outnumbered 2 to 1. Perhaps he considered scenarios in which his army could defeat the larger army: Do we have the high ground? Are there any aspects of the kingdom's topography that we can use to level the battlefield? Are our weapons superior to the enemy's? Jesus explained that if defeat was certain, the king could send a delegation to ask for peace (v. 32). Unlike the tower builder, the king was confronted with a decision outside the realm of his control; the enemy army was approaching, and the options were to fight or to request terms of peace. Yet, he still had to weigh the cost and value of his options to choose a wise course of action. The resulting impact of that decision necessitated careful consideration.

I imagine the listeners had begun to forget Jesus' initial rebuke of their motivations and expectations during the storytime portion of the teaching. Perhaps they scoffed at the idea of building a tower without first pricing the supplies, or maybe their minds wandered to the king's tactical dilemma, strategizing their own next move in a medieval

Day 11

game of Risk. But, Jesus snapped them back to attention with his closing remark: "So therefore, any one of *you* who does not renounce all that he has *cannot be my disciple* (v. 33, emphasis mine)." If there was any lingering doubt about what following Jesus would cost them, Jesus cleared it up. The word "renounce" means to "send away." Imagine filling a canoe with supplies and then pushing it out on the river, watching as it is slowly carried downstream. The decision to renounce those provisions has the potential for significant impact. In renouncing those provisions, you can no longer rely on them for sustenance, security, or safety. Making that choice only makes sense in light of a greater source of sustenance, security, and safety.

Jesus told the crowd they must renounce all that they have to be his disciple: family, personal safety, and everything else they had. We saw yesterday that "all" includes personal possessions and comfort. It includes our time and our financial resources. Picture the canoe again, and fill it with the people and things to which we tend to attach our significance: reputation, career, relationships, appearance, and bank statements. Think about where we often seek comfort: loved ones, coffee, stocked pantries, and hobbies. Consider where we often fix our hope for the future: 401Ks, political parties, gym memberships, education, and just more time on earth.

To be a disciple of Jesus, we must renounce *all* to follow him. Renouncing all is denying the world's attempts to provide significance, comfort, and hope for the future. It is ceasing our striving after the wind (Ecc 1:14) and believing God's word that all the world offers cannot profit or deliver our souls (1 Sam 12:21, Mk 8:36). Renouncing all is devoting our time to God, seeking first to build his kingdom and not to build our own. Renouncing all is valuing God himself above all others, directing the affections of our hearts to him. Renouncing all is surrendering our plans to God, submitting to his will for our lives – even if it means that we fail, suffer, or experience persecution.

In today's passage, Jesus confronted some who followed him for what he could provide for them on earth. He

Kingdom Residents

told them instead to count the cost. In doing so, Jesus gave a glimpse of the costs he endured to open for us the narrow door to God's kingdom. He, too, left his dwelling with God (Jn 1:1), taking on flesh to dwell among his created beings (Jn 1:14). Jesus renounced all the power and prestige of which he is infinitely worthy to "take the form of a servant" and "be born in the likeness of men (Phil 2:7)." He, too, left the comforts and stability of his earthly home, pursuing Kingdom ministry with no permanent place to lay his head (Lk 9:58). Jesus renounced the riches of heaven to become poor for our sakes, so that we "by his poverty might become rich (2 Cor 9:9)." He "humbled himself by becoming obedient to the point of death, even death on a cross (Phil 2:8)."

Jesus calls his disciples to take up their crosses. This is the life of costly discipleship. By his grace, we are enabled to become obedient to his will for our lives when we behold the glory of God, the treasure of Christ, and the riches of life in the kingdom. In Christ, we find our significance, we find our comfort, and we find our hope for the future.

Day 11

Food for Thought Hebrews 11 describes people who exhibited sacrificial faith in God and his promises despite the fact that they had not yet seen the promised Messiah (v. 13, 39-40), later revealed in Jesus. Read Hebrews 12:1-11. Reflect on what it cost Jesus to come to earth to rescue us. Notice his motivation in verse 2: "who for the joy that was set before him..." Then, read Philippians 3:7-11. Marvel at "the surpassing worth" (v. 8) of knowing Jesus Christ and being found in him. He is the joy set before us!

Faith in Action Think about the current source of your significance, comfort, and hope for the future. Are you holding tightly to a person, an outcome, a plan, or a possession? Is a family member or friend holding you back from following God wholeheartedly? Are you paralyzed by the need for security, unwilling to risk anything to follow Jesus? Have you become more attached to the good gifts in your life than the good God who gave them to you? Exposing barriers to discipleship may be painful, and renouncing them will cost you something here on earth. How does the joy of being found in Christ shape our perspective of the costs of discipleship?

Prayer In your prayer time today, rehearse the wonder of the gospel out loud. Thank God for rescuing you and adopting you into his family; for paying your sin debt and covering you in the righteousness of Christ. Praise him for the freedom and hope found in relationship with Christ. Then, ask God to give you the faith to believe the surpassing worth of Christ and to renounce all to follow him.

Day 12

Lampstand

Matthew 5:14-16

Even in the best of circumstances, everything just seems a little creepier at night. Before I committed to serve God as a pastor, I spent three years as a police officer in Chattanooga, TN. I worked the midnight shift for most of that time. As a result, I was always doing my job in some dark and scary places.

One night I received a call about a possible break in at a home in my district. It was one of those dark, winter nights where the wind howls and the cold holds you in its grasp like a vice. I arrived at an old farm-style house surrounded by huge oaks, their branches were being whipped into a frenzy by a strong, north wind. As I slipped through the darkness toward the back of the house, my senses were on high alert. Because I could barely see, I was listening for any sound of an intruder, either outside or inside the house.

As I turned the corner and stepped into the back yard, I heard the most ferocious barking. I spun towards the sound. All I could see was a large Doberman Pincher leaping towards me like a spectre of death. Its mouth was open, the large fangs clearly visible. Paralyzed by fear, I knew instinctively that this dog was going to kill me.

Suddenly, it was snatched back to earth as it reached the end of its chain, landing a few scant feet from

Kingdom Residents

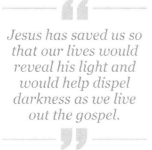

Jesus has saved us so that our lives would reveal his light and would help dispel darkness as we live out the gospel.

me. I stood trembling in the dark, praising God for his protection. As it turned out, there was no intruder. The elderly woman had been confused by the sound of the tree branches banging against her house. Still, I had encountered yet another example of the terrifying effects of darkness.

God didn't create us with the capacity to feel comfortable in darkness. Unlike some other creatures, our eyes are not designed to penetrate it. As a result, we're out of our element in the dark. We can't see to walk, work, or play unless we have access to some type of light. That is why I love headlights, floodlights, flashlights, lanterns, fires, or anything else that can penetrate darkness and help me see. Just as we were not created to function in darkness in the natural world, neither were we created to live in darkness in the spiritual world.

Today's short parable comes from Jesus' Sermon on the Mount. He is teaching another big crowd, and he reveals another identifying element of Kingdom residents. He said, "You are the light of the world. A city set on a hill cannot be hidden. Nor do people light a lamp and put it under a basket, but on a stand, and it gives light to all in the house. In the same way, let your light shine before others, so that they may see your good works and give glory to your Father who is in heaven."

The words "let your light shine" may feel rote to us. If you grew up in the church, you probably remember every verse of "This Little Light of Mine" and still picture Satan coming toward you with pursed lips ready to blow out your light. Even if you did not grow up in the church, you have likely seen at least one colorful social media post with fancy lettering and an encouraging mantra: "shine your light!" "Don't let anyone put out your light!" "Wherever you are, you shine!" What did Jesus mean when he called us the light of the world?

Day 12

Scripture tells us that Jesus, God in flesh, displayed the exact imprint of the nature of God (Heb 1:3), and that "God *is* light, and in him is no darkness at all (1 Jn 1:5, emphasis mine)." Likewise, the apostle John, under the inspiration of the Holy Spirit referred to Jesus as "the true light, which gives light to everyone (Jn 1:9)." Jesus himself said, "I am the light of the world. Whoever follows me will not walk in darkness, but will have the light of life (Jn 8:12)." When we become one of Jesus' disciples, he places his light within us – the very light of life.

Jesus used two analogies to help us understand this concept. First, he told us that a "city set on a hill cannot be hidden." In the ancient world, before the advances in modern warfare technology, the safest place to build a city was on a hill or mountain. In combat, those on the high ground always have the advantage. As a result, most well-conceived cities were built on an elevation. Also, the walls around the cities in Palestine were often constructed of pale shades of quarried rock. As a result, when the light of the sun reflected off of the stone, it produced a brilliant white appearance. Jesus was correct in his assessment that it's impossible to hide a city constructed of pale rocks and built on a mountain.

Second, Jesus told us that smart people use light for its intended purpose—to repel darkness. No one chooses to extinguish a light source in the dark; to do so would be foolish. Instead, like a city on a hill, the light is elevated so that it can have maximum impact at dispelling the darkness. Through these examples, we learn a key principle about Kingdom residency: Jesus has saved us so that our lives would reveal his light and would help dispel darkness as we live out the gospel.

What exactly is spiritual darkness, and how do we participate in God's work to dispel it? In the Bible, darkness is often used as an image for unbelief or an "un-

When we confess with our mouths that Jesus is Lord, and follow him despite the costs to our own glory, the testimony of our belief shines into the darkness.

Kingdom Residents

It is impossible to fellowship comfortably with the light and the darkness.

seeing" of revealed truth. In John 12, the apostle writes that though many saw Jesus perform miracles and signs, they still did not believe (v.37) he was who he said he was – the Son of God, the Messiah. Jesus said they remained in darkness through their unbelief (Jn 12:46). A life-giving truth is that it is Jesus who puts his light in us. We know that our salvation is by grace alone through faith. Since we were dead in our trespasses and sins, we had no capacity to open our own eyes to the truth of the gospel. The very fact that we see and recognize the Light of the World is a marvelous gift of grace.

Yet, the tension remains between the gracious gift of revelation and subsequent belief. The great tragedy is that some in Jesus' crowd did believe he was the Messiah, yet still they "did not confess it, so that they would not be put out of the synagogue (Jn 12:42)." They counted the cost and chose not to follow Jesus because "they loved the glory that comes from man more than the glory that comes from God (v. 43)." When by God's grace we confess with our mouths that Jesus is Lord, and follow him despite the costs to our own glory, the testimony of our belief shines into the darkness.

As we have seen, costly belief and confession has the potential for great impact in our lives here on earth. As a result, we may be tempted to become comfortable with the darkness, favoring more of an "under the radar" approach to the light of Christ in us. Maybe we don't want to make others feel different or bad. Maybe we don't want to be labeled or cut off from the rest of the group. Maybe we are afraid of missing out on "the fun" that the world seems to offer. Maybe we think we can occupy both the light and the darkness. But, James tells us that "friendship with the world is enmity with God," and "whoever wishes to be a friend of the world makes himself an enemy of God (Jam 4:4)." Likewise, John wrote, "If we say we have fel-

Day 12

lowship with him while we walk in darkness, we lie and do not practice the truth (1 Jn 1:6)."

It is impossible to fellowship comfortably with the light and the darkness. How we choose to live testifies to the reality of our belief and confession: our responses to adversity and inconvenience; how we talk about others; our sexual ethic; how we spend our time; our speech; how we spend our money. How we live reveals whom we love. John wrote, "Do not love the world or the things in the world. If anyone loves the world, the love of the Father is not in him (1 Jn 2:15)." We cannot comfortably fellowship with the world and with God. An illuminated city on a hill cannot be hidden, and a lamp that has been lit and elevated will give light to all in the house.

In his mercy, the Holy Spirit convicts God's children when they live in friendship with the world. In his love, God disciplines his children for their good that they might repent. In his grace, God forgives his children when we confess (1 Jn 1:9) and restores us to comfortable fellowship with him. He enables us not only to walk in the light as he is in the light, but also to shine the light of Christ into a world that is passing away. And, he gives us glimpses of the surpassing glory of God that we will inherit in Christ: "The sun shall be no more your light by day, nor for brightness shall the moon give you light, but the LORD will be your everlasting light, and your God will be your glory. Your sun shall no more go down, nor your moon withdraw itself; for the LORD will be your everlasting light, and your days of mourning shall be ended. Your people shall all be righteous; they shall possess the land forever, the branch of my planting, the work of my hands, that I might be glorified (Is 60:19-21)."

We have been saved for a glorious future, and in the meantime, we get to share in a glorious purpose: to let our light shine before others so that they might see our good works and give glory to our Father who is in heaven (Mt 5:16).

Kingdom Residents

Food for Thought — Read Isaiah 60. Notice the prophet Isaiah's references to seeing and being light. How do glimpses of our eternal future give us confidence and joy to shine the light of Christ in this life? For additional encouragement, search and listen to "O Church Arise (Arise, Shine)" by Keith and Kristyn Getty ft. Chris Tomlin. "When faced with trials on every side, we know the outcome is secure. And Christ will have the prize for which He died: an inheritance of nations."

Faith in Action — Every authentic disciple may be described in one of three ways: 1) his light is covered by disobedience, and cannot be seen in the darkness;
2) her light is partially covered by disobedience, and only a small glimmer of light can be seen; 3) his light is shining brightly into the darkness for all to see. Which one are you today? Why would you describe yourself this way? What needs to change so that your light can shine brightly as God desires?

Prayer

Today, talk with God about your spiritual light. Spend time in confession and repentance of any dimness or covering. Then, pray about some specific ways that you want to reflect God's light today. Ask God to help you see this life through eternal eyes and to love his glory more than your own.

Day 13

Soils

Mark 4:1-20

My wife Lyla and I have attended numerous timeshare presentations over the years. They give us a great opportunity to spend a weekend exploring new places. Of course, the downside of the timeshare weekend is the two hours I donate to hear the sales pitch. But for me, it's a small price to pay for a free weekend. When you attend a timeshare presentation, you choose a time to tour the facility and meet with a sales representative. When you arrive, however, you discover that you're grouped with about 10 other couples that are there to tour the resort as well. The last time I attended a timeshare presentation, I observed my fellow explorers. I would put them into four categories.

The first group I observed was the "No Thanks" group. These are the folks like me who are attending solely for the free weekend, the free breakfast, and the complimentary $50 gift card. They have absolutely no intention of buying a timeshare. They've got their faces set like stone—they're not about to give one indication that they're even remotely interested. They want to take the tour and then get on with their weekend plans.

Then, I observed the "This is Awesome" crowd. They're easy to spot. It's their first time to visit a timeshare presentation, and they're excited about discovering what it's all about. They tour the rooms, and they're amazed by

Kingdom Residents

Spiritual fruit is the evidence of spiritual transformation.

how cool they are. When it's time to look at the big book containing all of the places they can trade their week to visit, their eyes dance with anticipation. But then they see the price to buy a week, and their enthusiasm begins to wane. And even though the manager offers them a "reduced" price, it's still too much. They're interested, but they're unable to buy a timeshare.

Next, I observed the "This is an Option" crowd. There are always one or two couples at the timeshare presentation who look out of place. Clearly, they have money. They don't need a free weekend; they look like they could own the resort! Yet, here they are. They appraise the resort with practiced eyes. They've stayed in many places nicer than this, so they're not easily impressed. They're curious about the potential of trading their unit, and they look to see if there are resorts in the places they like to travel. When the sales representative shares the price, they don't even flinch—money is no problem here. For these couples, the issue is one of priority. They already have so many other options in their lives; they must decide whether they really want to add one more thing to the list. After some thoughtful dialogue, they decide to pass. They're intrigued, but they're unwilling to buy a timeshare.

The final group is the "All In" crowd. These are the folks who came prepared to buy a timeshare if they liked the property. Perhaps they grew up in a family that enjoyed using timeshares, or perhaps they had vacationed in one with a friend. Either way, they're at the presentation on a mission. They're interested in all of the amenities at the resort and intrigued by the possibility of vacationing at other resorts in the future. After haggling with the sales representative, they reach a price point that works for their budget. They like the place, the perks, and the price. They're all in. They buy it, use it, and enjoy it for years to come.

Day 13

What is the difference between these four groups of people? They all went to the same place, heard the same pitch, and had the same opportunity to buy a timeshare. Yet only one of the four made the decision to buy one. Why? The answer is simple—only one was willing to accept the offer to buy one. In Mark 4:1-20, Jesus told a parable that examines similar questions about the human heart. In this parable, a farmer sowed seed onto his land. Some fell on the hard path, some fell on rocky ground, some fell into the thorny hedgerow, and some fell on the good soil and yielded a crop. The disciples were wrestling with the interpretation, so Jesus helped them.

The seed represents the truth of the gospel, and the different soils represent the different conditions of the human heart. When the seed falls on a hard heart, Satan can swiftly carry it away—the ground is too hard to receive the seed. This is the "No Thanks" group. Their hearts are hard, impenetrable, and impervious to their need for the gospel. They want to escape from its truth as quickly as possible.

When the seed falls on a rocky heart, it is received immediately with interest. This is the person who is a seeker, always looking for another trinket to add to her worldview collection. Initially, she responds to the message of the gospel with joy—maybe this is finally the thing that will work in her life. She represents the "This is Awesome" crowd. She continues to investigate, but then she discovers that the gospel makes too many demands upon her life. She must choose Christ alone; he will not be numbered among the many gods of her life. This is too much for her to accept, and so she falls away.

When the seed falls on a thorny heart, it is received with cautious optimism. This hearer is measured in his response to the gospel, just like he is to everything else in his life. He makes his choices based upon the demands of his calendar; he is far too busy to waste time on nonessentials. Still,

God has not only gifted us and called us to serve him; he has also empowered us to serve him by giving us the Holy Spirit.

Kingdom Residents

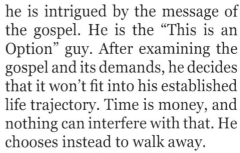

> The more we learn about our identity as Kingdom residents, the more we should give God glory for inviting us to share in this treasured inheritance.

he is intrigued by the message of the gospel. He is the "This is an Option" guy. After examining the gospel and its demands, he decides that it won't fit into his established life trajectory. Time is money, and nothing can interfere with that. He chooses instead to walk away.

When the seed falls on a receptive heart, however, something amazing happens. This person is both interested and intrigued by its message of grace and forgiveness. Rather than seeing the gospel as another self-help strategy or a rung on the ladder of success, she sees it for what it is—a life changing offer of hope. She hears the gospel, accepts the gospel, and begins to live the gospel. She is "All In" in her relationship with Christ, and her life yields an abundant harvest.

Jesus described four groups of people. All heard the same gospel and had the same opportunity to respond. Three turned their backs and walked away, content to pursue the false promises of a broken world. But one responded to the gospel by faith and was forever changed. What, ultimately, reveals the condition of their hearts? It is the absence or presence of spiritual fruit. Through this parable, Jesus reveals that spiritual fruit is the evidence of spiritual transformation. Once he rescues us and puts his light in us, our lives will bear fruit, "thirtyfold and sixtyfold and a hundredfold (v. 20)."

Jesus used the image of fruit often in his teaching. In the last section of our study, we will examine specific fruits of Kingdom residents that Jesus reveals through his parables. Before we begin examining different fruits, we must understand the role fruit plays in our identity as Kingdom residents. Over the next few days, we will see that our spiritual fruit is planted by God and produced by God. We will be reminded that our religious performance does not save us; rather, our growing love for God and our willing service to God are born out of our gratitude for

Day 13

salvation. Finally, we will see that while our works don't save us, they will be tested. God has not only gifted us and called us to serve him; he has also empowered us to serve him by giving us the Holy Spirit. The more we learn about our identity as Kingdom residents, the more we should give God glory for inviting us to share in this treasured inheritance.

Kingdom Residents

Food for Thought

If you are in Christ today, you have a story of hearing the truth of the gospel, accepting it, and bearing fruit. Think about your story – who shared with you? Did the condition of your heart change from hard, rocky, or thorny to receptive? Thank God for how he pursued you and softened your heart to receive his offer of salvation. Consider reaching out to believers in your story who shared the truth with you, or spend time thanking God for their faithfulness.

Faith in Action

Jesus said, "each tree is known by its own fruit (Lk 6:44)." We know that God is the author and judge of each person's relationship with him, and without the righteousness of Christ given to us, none could stand before him. Each of us is in need of his mercy every day. By his grace, God grows us into the likeness of his Son as we seek him. If someone looked at your life today – your time, your money, your relationships, your words – would they see Jesus in you? Likewise, as you consider the fruit of your closest friends and family members, pray for opportunities to join God's work of sowing gospel seeds and sharing the hope of Christ with them today.

Prayer

Start your prayer time today by thanking God for revealing the truth of the gospel to you. Thank him for planting you in his kingdom. Then, ask for the faith to follow Jesus today and to point others to him. Finally, ask for opportunities to share the gospel today, and ask the Holy Spirit to give you the words to say and to allow the seeds to fall on receptive hearts.

Day 14

Mustard Seed

Luke 13:18-20

Morning Glories are known for their pretty flowers which bloom every morning. Their vines grow rapidly, embracing other vegetation, ultimately covering them with a blanket of color. When I see the rapid growth and beauty of Morning Glories on my farm, I always think of the particular parables that Jesus told in our text for today.

It appears that someone listening to Jesus asked him what the kingdom of God was like. In the first section of our study, we saw Jesus consistently flip audience expectations in answer to that question. In today's parable, Jesus said that the kingdom of God "is like a grain of mustard seed that a man took and sowed in his garden, and it grew and became a tree, and the birds of the air made nests in its branches (v. 19)." Jesus' audience would have been familiar with the mustard plant. Though its seed is one of the smallest on earth, it can grow into a large tree where birds can rest and roost.

As Jesus was talking, he thought of another illustration: the kingdom of God is "like leaven that a woman took and hid in three measures of flour, until it was all leavened (v. 21)." Jesus' audience would have known that "a little leaven leavens the whole lump (Gal 5:9)." Once yeast is added to flour, the resulting fermentation process allows the dough to rise before it is baked into bread. In both of

Kingdom Residents

> Misunderstanding the source of our spiritual fruit can lead us into the guilt, shame, or self-righteousness that God has freed us from through Christ.

these illustrations, Jesus was describing important facets of the kingdom of God: that it is always expanding and its growth cannot be stopped. Jesus was also adding to our understanding of his role in establishing and growing his kingdom.

Understanding God's role in Kingdom growth is critical to understanding our role as Kingdom residents. We have seen the costly and valuable nature of residency in God's kingdom and how our identity as disciples shapes how we live in the world. We have heard Jesus give commands that reveal our role in discipleship: Let your light shine; take up your cross; renounce all; follow me. We have read Jesus' litmus test: "you will recognize them by their fruits (Mt 7:20)." Yet, depending on your church background, family history, and personal bents, studying spiritual fruit can serve as a pitfall. Learning about the attributes that signify our residency in God's kingdom should bring us great joy, but misunderstanding the *source* of our spiritual fruit can lead us into the guilt, shame, or self-righteousness that God has freed us from through Christ.

In today's parables, we find encouragement as followers of Jesus who still battle sin in this present age. We find freedom from the self-striving which leads only to pride or despair. We see two glorious truths about God's role in the work of spiritual transformation and Kingdom expansion. The first is this: God plants spiritual fruit. In the first illustration, a man plants the mustard seed, which later grows into a tree. In the second, a woman adds the leavening agent to dough, which allows it to ferment and expand. In both cases, an external agent initiates the process of transformation.

God, in his boundless love toward us, opens our eyes to recognize our need for rescue. He reveals our need to confess our sin and place our faith in Jesus' death and

Day 14

resurrection. When we believe and confess, he is faithful to forgive and to cleanse us of our sin. Not only does he expunge our sin debt, but he also gives us the righteousness of Jesus so that when we stand before God, we bear Jesus' perfect record. We are justified – made righteous – through our faith in Jesus alone. Our hope for justification rests firmly on Jesus. Why, then, would we transfer our hope for spiritual transformation onto ourselves?

Paul speaks to this possibility in Galatians 5. He is calling out members of the early church whom Paul said had been "running well (v. 7)." They had placed their faith in Jesus' victory for salvation. However, some were now adding to faith in Jesus the physical requirement of circumcision, an Old Covenant sign (v. 3). Paul does not take this offense lightly. In adding to Jesus' saving work, he said, "You are severed from Christ, you who would be justified by the law; you have fallen away from grace (v.4)."

Do you think Paul's readers were shocked by his rebuke? Perhaps they thought that they would be commended for their extra dose of righteousness and human effort. Instead, Paul asked, "Who hindered you from obeying the truth? This persuasion is not from him who calls you. A little leaven leavens the whole lump (vv. 7-9)." Sound familiar? Paul doesn't place self-sanctification in a different category from self-justification. Attempting to earn our own salvation *or* to produce our own righteousness severs us from Christ.

It is here that we see the second glorious truth about God's role in spiritual transformation: God produces spiritual fruit. Think about the mustard seed again. To become a tree, the seed must be planted. With time and nourishment, the seed must undergo significant transformation from seed to stalk to trunk and boughs. The transformation of the seed into a tree capable of housing birds is ultimately dependent on

Our understanding of God's role in planting Kingdom residents and producing spiritual fruit should bring us into deep gratitude and peace.

Kingdom Residents

> *Our ability to bear fruit does not stem from our ability to conjure goodness. Fruit cannot will itself to grow.*

the water and sunlight it receives. We are similarly dependent on God both for our initial transformation from spiritually dead to spiritually alive and for our subsequent spiritual growth.

Twice in Matthew, Jesus said that trees can be known "by their fruits (7:16, 12:33)." Toward the end of his Sermon on the Mount, Jesus asked, "Are grapes gathered from thornbushes or figs from thistles? So, every healthy tree bears good fruit, but the diseased tree bears bad fruit (Mt 7:16-17)." The type and quality of the tree determines the type and quality of fruit produced. Paul said that the fruit of the flesh is evident: "sexual immorality, impurity, sensuality, idolatry, sorcery, enmity, strife, jealousy, fits of anger, rivalries, dissensions, divisions, envy, drunkenness, orgies, and things like these (Gal 5:19-21)." These external fruits of inward "desires of the flesh" (v. 16) reveal a tree plagued with disease and at odds with the Spirit of God (v. 17).

Thankfully, for believers, our tree is Christ! In John 15, Jesus said, "I am the true vine (v. 1)." He lived a perfect, sinless life. He only ever bore good fruit. When Jesus rescues us, we are grafted into his tree – "we are the branches (v.5)" – which enables us to bear good fruit. Our ability to bear fruit does not stem from our ability to conjure goodness. Fruit cannot will itself to grow. Rather, our ability to bear fruit stems from the goodness that is in our vine. The quality of the fruit depends entirely on the quality of the tree. When we read Paul's list of spiritual fruit, then, we need not despair. Our vine displays perfect "love, joy, peace, patience, kindness, goodness, faithfulness, gentleness, self-control (Gal 5:22-23)."

The call, then, is to abide in him. Jesus said, "Abide in me, and I in you. As the branch cannot bear fruit by itself, unless it abides in the vine, neither can you, unless you abide in me...Whoever abides in me...bears much fruit (vv. 4-5)." Our lives bear the good fruits of our vine when

Day 14

we abide in him. In step with the Spirit, we can display Christ's love, joy, peace, and self-control to those around us. When those fruits cease, it is not because we failed to strive hard enough; we could never be good enough or righteous enough to produce spiritual fruit in our own strength. Rather, we fail to produce good fruit when we cease to abide in the true vine.

What, then, does it mean to abide? How can we daily remain "in step with the Spirit (Gal 5:25)"? Abiding is putting our hope for justification in Jesus' finished work on the cross. Abiding is putting our hope for sanctification in Jesus' perfect righteousness given to us. Abiding is putting our hope for ultimate restoration in Jesus' promises to fulfill his good purposes for us. When we put our hope in *his* work on our behalf, we will bear good fruit because our tree is Good.

Our understanding of God's role in planting Kingdom residents and producing spiritual fruit should bring us into deep gratitude and peace. God does the work of planting, transforming, and growing us into his likeness. Apart from him, we can do nothing. Fear, guilt, and pride melt away in view of that truth.

With joy, let us hear and heed Jesus' call to abide in him today, and let us look again to our glorious future, for God's work of planting seeds and transforming hearts cannot be stopped. Like the mustard seed, his kingdom began very small with Jesus, his disciples, and a few hundred Jewish believers. Yet, it began to grow, first slowly and then with greater speed following Pentecost. From that time to this, over the span of twenty centuries, the kingdom of God on earth has grown to include millions of Christ followers. Like the leavened lump, the Kingdom will continue to expand until it covers the earth during the millennial reign of Jesus Christ on earth. What a gift to be a resident in the growing, transforming, unstoppable kingdom of God.

Food for Thought Consider your perceptions about spiritual fruit. Have you ever viewed your own efforts as the source of the fruits of the Spirit? When we look to ourselves as the source of spiritual fruit production, we can easily teeter-totter between guilt and pride, depending on how we feel about our performance on a given day. Yet, Jesus said, "apart from me you can do nothing (Jn 15:5)." How do those words free us from a performance-based perspective of spiritual fruit? Read Galatians 5 in light of Jesus' call to abide in him, the true source of all spiritual fruit.

Faith in Action Failing to abide in Jesus often looks like attaching our hopes to our own performance, our expectations of other people, or our desire for earthly things. If something angers or frustrates you today, ask, "Am I looking for hope in this? What do I expect this person or thing to provide for me?" Then, rehearse who you are in Christ and what secure hope you possess in him.

Prayer In your prayer time, ask God to reveal your source of fruit. If you find yourself bearing diseased fruit, run to the merciful arms of your Lord. He always forgives us when we confess. Ask God to empower you to abide in Jesus today that you might look like him, honor him, and point others to him.

Day 15

Kind Money Lender

Luke 7:36-50

Gratitude seems to be in short supply today. From the time we're children, many of us develop a sense of entitlement. Most of us grew up as children who had everything provided for us—our house, food, clothes, toys, and more. Because we don't have the means to understand why all of these things are simply given to us, we can begin to believe that we must deserve them. As a result, we have a hard time expressing gratitude when we're children. Sadly, we often carry that same mindset into our adult years.

Entitlement in adulthood can manifest in our jobs, relationships, and even our faith. Sometimes entitlement looks like comparing our performances to others and finding ourselves more deserving of appreciation or blessing. Sometimes entitlement looks like questioning the appreciation or blessing others receive. In either case, it is difficult to feel or express gratitude when we feel entitled. Yesterday, we were reminded of God's role in Kingdom expansion and in our own spiritual transformation. Today's parable reveals the proper response to God's saving and transforming work in us.

Jesus was teaching in Galilee when a Pharisee named Simon invited him to dinner. Simon had heard much about Jesus; namely, that he spent time with tax collectors and sinners, yet still the people were calling him

Kingdom Residents

He who is forgiven little, loves little.

a prophet. He had heard Jesus teach, and as much as he hated to admit it, this teacher was gifted. But who was he, really?

Jesus was talking with Simon and the other guests when a most unusual thing happened. Suddenly, a woman appeared in the room and knelt near Jesus' feet. But she wasn't just any woman—she was a prostitute. Broken and weeping, she began to wash Jesus' feet, using her hair as a towel to dry them. Then, when his feet were clean, she anointed them with a costly ointment.

Can you imagine the look on Simon the Pharisee's face when she walked into the room? The Pharisees spent their time looking down on women like this, not inviting them into their homes. Simon doesn't speak to the woman—he's probably speechless! But, his mind was working feverishly. He watched Jesus and was surprised by his willingness to let this woman wash his feet. He began to reason through a simple syllogism. He thought, "If Jesus was a prophet he would know what kind of woman is touching him. Clearly, Jesus doesn't know what kind of woman this is. So, Jesus is not a prophet." I'm sure Simon was pleased with the conclusion he reached. The Pharisees had been trying to figure out who Jesus was and why he did the things that he did (Lk 5:27- 32), and now he could tell his pals that Jesus was a fraud.

Jesus was watching Simon at the same time from the other side of table. He knew exactly what Simon was thinking about the woman. And, he knew the exact moment when Simon reached the false conclusion about him. Looking at Simon, Jesus said, "Simon, I have something to say to you. And, he answered, 'Say it, Teacher (v. 40).'"

Jesus began to tell Simon a parable about a moneylender who was owed money by two men. The first man owed him 500 denarii (approximately $30,000 today). The second man owed him 50 denarii (approximately $2,500 today). While they owed different amounts, they

Day 15

had one thing in common—neither of them had the money to repay their loans. In Jesus' day, men in this situation were sent to debtor's prisons. There, they would be hired out to work, and their wages would be paid to the moneylender. Their families would suffer greatly during this time. In Jesus' parable, the moneylender made an unexpected decision; rather than condemn the debtors to this fate, he chose to forgive the debts of both men.

Jesus let his parable hang in the air while he watched Simon's face. Then, he asked him this question: "Which of them will love him more?" It was a simple question with a simple answer, but Simon squirmed in his seat. Finally he stammered, "The one, I suppose, for whom he cancelled the larger debt." Jesus reply was swift, "You have judged rightly (vv. 42-43)." Then, he began to speak to Simon about the actions of the woman. He said, "Simon, you didn't wash my feet when I arrived, but this woman has washed my feet with her tears. You didn't kiss me when I arrived, but this woman has kissed my feet. You didn't anoint my head with oil, but she has poured ointment on my feet. You've done nothing that would say you care for me, but she has demonstrated her love." Then, Jesus made an amazing statement: "He who is forgiven little, loves little (v. 47)." Here, Jesus speaks to an important aspect of Kingdom residency: an appropriate understanding of our forgiveness will lead to an appropriate appreciation for our forgiveness.

Notice how gratitude and love are linked in today's parable. Though both debtors must have felt relieved, awed, and grateful to the moneylender, the one who owed more money would naturally feel more relieved, awed, and grateful. He loved the moneylender to a greater degree because he understood how much the debt would cost him to pay and how much the debt would cost the lender to forgive. In God's economy, all sinners bear the same debt. It is humans

When we think about what we are given on the basis of Christ's performance, we must pour out gratitude and love.

Kingdom Residents

In God's economy, all sinners bear the same debt. It is humans who try to itemize sins from "budget" to "high end."

who try to itemize sins from "budget" to "high end." Simon demonstrated this tendency. Compared to sinners like this woman, his life looked pretty good; but, he failed to understand sin from God's perspective. Like the woman, he was a debtor to God because of his sin, and he was equally unable to pay the debt that he owed. Only God – the one ultimately sinned against – was capable of forgiving the sin debt that he owed. Unfortunately, his pride blinded him to the reality of his own lostness.

On the other hand, the woman washing Jesus' feet knew only too well the gravity of her situation. We don't know where she had encountered Jesus and heard his message of hope. Unlike Simon, she was broken over her sin, and responded in repentance and faith. Jesus confirmed this when he shared these words of grace with her, "Your sins are forgiven...Your faith has saved you; go in peace (v. 48, 50)." Her rightful responses to the forgiveness extended to her were gratitude and love. Had she tried to earn God's favor in her own strength, she might have sold the alabaster flask and the ointment it contained to purchase offerings or to give away to the poor. Instead, out of the abundance of her gratitude and love, she poured out a costly offering on the feet of Jesus.

Her response to Jesus' mercy and grace toward her help us understand our rightful response. Like Simon, our hearts are quick to compare our spiritual performances. We can so easily be tempted to view our sin debt as smaller than others'. When we do that, we diminish the blood of Jesus spilled for us. Holding up our own works of righteousness severs us from the power of his righteousness. As children of God and residents in his kingdom, this is far from what we desire. To combat entitlement, we need God's grace to remember that salvation is the result of repentance and faith – not religious performance. Because when we think about what we deserve on the basis of *our*

Day 15

performance, we rightly think of death. When we, instead, think about what we are given on the basis of Christ's performance, we must pour out our gratitude and love.

So, remember the extent of God's grace poured out on us. Remember who we were – like the debtors in the parable, we held loans we could never afford to pay back. Our sin so permeated our lives that even our best efforts earned us wages of death (Rom 6:23). Remember what God did – in the kindness of his mercy toward us, he forgave our sins and gave us the Holy Spirit as a guarantee that Christ's payment on the cross was accepted on our behalf (Col 2:14). Remember what he has promised – in his grace, we not only escape debtor's prison; we also are given residency in God's kingdom and all the treasures of Christ's inheritance. Remember and rejoice.

Kingdom Residents

Food for Thought

It is easy to develop an entitlement mentality in our lives, including our spiritual journey. Today, spend time remembering the grace that God poured into your life when he drew you to faith in Jesus Christ. Read Ephesians 1-2, taking note of the depth of your lostness before you believed and confessed Christ. Notice all of the gifts God gave you in him.

Faith in Action

The woman in today's text demonstrated her gratitude and love for Jesus by serving him. This is a great model for us to follow. True love serves. Today, look for opportunities to serve Jesus by serving others. Look for ways to serve your spouse, family, friends, co-workers, or even a stranger. God always blesses our decision to serve others.

Prayer

In today's prayer time, express your gratitude to God for his grace in providing forgiveness for your sins. Ask him to expose any areas of entitlement and to help you remember all of the different blessings he has given you. And, ask him for opportunities to demonstrate your love for him through serving others.

Day 16

The Talents

Matthew 25:14-30

I'll never forget when my Grandmother died. She was 100 years old and ready to be with Jesus, so I viewed her passing with great joy. The true challenge came after. I was the executor of her will, so the responsibility fell to me to make her final arrangements and disperse her requested items to the family. Rarely have I felt such pressure. Even though she was gone, she had entrusted me with all of her possessions, and I knew that she wanted me to manage them well. I felt the weight of her presence throughout the entire process, and I believe she would be pleased with how I oversaw the task.

Jesus was nearing the time of his crucifixion when he told a similar story to his disciples. The story begins just before a successful business owner departed for a lengthy trip. Knowing that he wouldn't be on site to manage his affairs, he made the necessary arrangements for the oversight of his business during his absence. To that end, he selected three of his most trusted employees to manage different aspects of the business while he was away. He called in his first employee and made him manager over the majority of the business. He was in charge of managing five talents of silver, the equivalent of 2.5 million dollars in today's currency values. Then, he called in his second employee and made him manager over two talents of silver,

Kingdom Residents

God plans to return to assess what we've done with what we've been given.

the equivalent of 1 million dollars in today's currency values. Finally, he called in his third employee and made him manager over one talent of silver, the equivalent of five hundred thousand dollars in today's currency values. Remember, each of these employees was handpicked for this task on the basis of their character and assigned management roles on the basis of their ability. When this process was complete, the business manager left on his trip.

Can you imagine what those men felt as they watched their boss leave? I'm sure the weight of responsibility fell on them with a thud. They were now responsible for the oversight, management, and investment of all of their boss' financial resources. Prior to this, they lived and worked in that comfortable place where their responsibilities were limited to their own personal assignments and outcomes. They didn't have to worry about whether the business succeeded or failed—that was their boss' concern. But suddenly, all of that had changed. They were now responsible for the success or failure of the business, and that changed everything. Consider how Jesus' parable in Matthew 25 might look in today's business world.

The dust from their boss' caravan was just settling on the road outside their business when the first employee went to work. He didn't know how long his boss would be away, but he wanted the manufacturing and sales departments to be in tip-top shape when he returned. After all, he was responsible for more than half of the business' net worth. Immediately, he began scheduling meetings with the employees he managed, contacting suppliers, and connecting with customers. Soon, his area was humming smoothly. He was certain that his master would be pleased. As time passed, his sector raced forward on all cylinders. In time, he had doubled the money his boss had placed under his care. Employee number two, who watched his colleague with interest, was inspired to lead in a similar fashion. He

Day 16

was over research and development. He began to consider new areas of industry that could be incorporated into the existing business. He located and purchased a couple of startups, hired and trained new workers, and launched new products. These new arms were then absorbed into his fellow manager's area of manufacturing and sales. As a result of his hard work and creative thinking, he, too, doubled the money his boss had entrusted to him.

Employee number three observed his fellow managers. However, he quickly convinced himself that he wasn't capable of leading with that kind of passion or creativity. After all, he had been placed in charge of advertising, and he had the smallest budget of the three. Everyone already knew about their business, so maintaining the status quo in public relations was the safest route to take. They had already generated enough money to sustain the advertising department. The quickest way to lose money was to get creative in advertising. What if he designed a new ad campaign and it flopped? He knew if he lost money his boss would be furious. So, he structured his budget to spend only that which he knew would be replaced by their current advertising strategies. Hey, his department wouldn't make any money, but they wouldn't lose any either.

Months passed, until word reached the plant that the boss was arriving later that week. The entire company raced to make sure that everything was in pristine order. The offices were cleaned, the warehouses were organized, and the grounds were swept and cleaned. When the boss arrived, his three managers met him at the door. There were great expressions of kindness and affection shared between the boss and his chosen managers. This was a happy and long-anticipated reunion.

Jesus did not command his servants to accomplish a task without first imbuing them with the power required to carry out the task.

Once they were back in their boss' office, they got down to business. You can imagine the anticipation felt by the owner. He

While our work as Kingdom managers does not save us, it will be assessed.

wasted no time in assessing the condition of his business. He had risked much by leaving his entire fortune in the hands of his managers, but he had confidence in their ability to do the job. He eagerly awaited their reports.

One by one, the men stood to make their reports. The first employee completed his overview and demonstrated that he had doubled the money under his control. Immediately, his boss leaped to his feet and embraced him. "Well done! You are such a good and faithful manager. I have a huge bonus for you!" When it was his turn, the second employee took his place behind the podium and began his presentation. Slide by slide passed by until he reached the end. He, too, revealed that he had doubled the money in his department. Once again, the owner leaped to his feet and embraced him. "Well done! You are such a good and faithful manager. I have a huge bonus for you!"

Finally, the third employee moved slowly to the podium. He suddenly felt quite nervous about his report—he didn't even have a presentation. He cleared his throat and began with a number of disclaimers. "I'm thankful for the opportunity you gave me. Um, advertising is a tricky business—you never really know what will motivate people to purchase something. Uh, I had the smallest budget, and the last thing I wanted to do was lose money. So…" Slowly, he passed a simple profit and loss form out to the others in the meeting. The room fell silent as they read the statement. The report showed zero sum growth in his department. Finally, he spoke again. "I'm pleased to say that my department didn't lose a dime of your money." Quietly, he walked over to his chair and was seated.

All eyes turned towards the owner. His eyes burrowed into those of the third manager. Slowly, the owner's face grew crimson, while the veins in his neck began to throb. He sat silently for what seemed like days. Finally, he spoke in measured tones, his eyes blazing like a fire.

Day 16

"You are a worthless and lazy manager. Clearly, you did not heed my instructions. Of course, I hate losing money, especially when it results from poor stewardship. The least you could have done is invest some of it so that I would've gained some interest. As it is, you have cost me untold amounts of money and influence for my business because of your foolishness." At this point the owner turned to his first manager. "I'm moving all of his area under your leadership group. I know that you'll know what to do with it." Then he turned his hardened gaze back on his third manager. "Because I love and care about you, I'm not going to fire you; you will remain one of my employees. However, not only is there no reward bonus for you, but also you will no longer be one of my managers. You will report to the warehouse floor tomorrow morning, where daily you will mourn past choices and your lack of future opportunities."

In our study of Kingdom residency, we have seen how God rescues and redeems us, planting us in his kingdom. We have studied how our service to God stems from our gratitude and love for him, and how our light and fruit flow from abiding in Christ, the source of our righteousness. Today's parable reveals key truths about God's role as King and our purpose as Kingdom residents.

First, we see that Jesus is the owner and King of God's kingdom. In his final words before ascending, Jesus said, "All authority in heaven and on earth has been given to me (Mt 28:18)." Second, like the boss who entrusted his servants with talents and a task, Jesus commanded us to participate in the work of his kingdom. After he explained his authority, he said, "Go therefore and make disciples (Mt 28:19)." We are not passive residents in God's kingdom; we are managers of the resources entrusted to us. There is no "opt out" plan; we are tasked with investing in God's kingdom. Third, God does not ask us to carry out Jesus' management plan in our own strength. Think of the boss in today's parable. Before leaving, he imbued his chosen managers with the authority and resources required to complete the assignment. In the same way, Jesus gave his

Kingdom Residents

servants the Holy Spirit to empower them for the mission. In his ascension account, Luke wrote,

> [Jesus] said to them . . . 'You will receive power when the Holy Spirit has come upon you, and you will be my witnesses in Jerusalem and in all Judea and Samaria, and to the end of the earth.' And when he had said these things, as they were looking on, he was lifted up, and a cloud took him out of their sight. (Acts 1:8-9)

Jesus did not command his servants to accomplish a task without first imbuing them with the power required to carry out the task. Through the Spirit, Jesus promised to be with them "always, to the end of the age (Mt 28:20)." Scripture tells us that we who are in Christ are indwelled with the Holy Spirit (Jn 14:25-26) who likewise fills, gifts, resources, and empowers us to labor in the kingdom until Christ's return.

Fourth, while our work as Kingdom managers does not save us, it will be assessed. Like the business owner in today's parable, God plans to return to assess what we've done with what we've been given. Notice what Paul wrote in 2 Corinthians 5: "For we must all appear before the judgment seat of Christ, so that each of us may receive what is due for what he has done in the body, whether good or evil (v. 10)." Consider, also, 1 Corinthians 3:11-15,

> For no one can lay a foundation other than that which is laid, which is Jesus Christ. Now if anyone builds on the foundation with gold, silver, precious stones, wood, hay, straw—each one's work will become manifest, for the Day will disclose it, because it will be revealed by fire, and the fire will test what sort of work each one has done. If the work that anyone has built on the foundation survives, he will receive a reward. If anyone's work is

Day 16

burned up, he will suffer loss, though he himself will be saved, but only as through fire.

Here, Paul emphasizes that how we spend our resources on earth is not our salvation; instead, how we invest our resources will be tested by God, who entrusted the resources to us. The testing of our management will determine God's response. In the parable, the manager who accepted the talent and did nothing to invest or multiply received a stern rebuke: "You are a worthless and lazy manager." What great sorrow to hear those words from Christ our King. Jesus described the profound sorrow of the lazy manager as "weeping and gnashing of teeth (v. 30)."

It's sobering to reflect on this parable. God is serious about how we live as Kingdom residents. Yet, it's comforting as well. It is comforting because we see yet again that our salvation is not contingent on our own works. Our concern is not to amass enough talents to bring to our King in order to be accepted on the basis of our merit. Rather, because he has chosen and accepted us on the basis of Jesus' merit, he empowers us with the Holy Spirit and entrusts us with gifts and earthly resources to live and share the gospel with those around us.

It is comforting because we find a glimpse of God's response when we participate in his kingdom work. In the parable, the faithful managers heard, "Well done, good and faithful servant." What a delight to hear those words from Christ our King. The faithful managers not only received an affirming word; they also received more to manage: "You have been faithful over a little; I will set you over much (v. 21)." Similarly, we will be rewarded for "doing the will of God from the heart, rendering services with a good will as to the Lord and not to man (Eph 6:6-7)."

God wants us to faithfully serve him with joyful hearts, laboring in his kingdom until we hear him say, "Well done, good and faithful servant!"

Kingdom Residents

  Finally, reflecting on this parable is comforting because we see that we will not be judged for what others do in God's kingdom. Make no mistake – God wants us to invest the gifts and resources he has given to us for his glory, but God is in control over whether we have five talents, two talents, or one talent. He will never expect us to do more than he has equipped us to do. The manager who had two talents could never produce the results of the manager with five talents, but the owner didn't require that of him. He asked him to be faithful and multiply his resources. That's exactly what he did, and that's why he got the same affirmation and reward as the manager with five talents. It's the same with us. God wants us to serve him faithfully with joyful hearts, laboring in his kingdom until we hear him say, "Well done, good and faithful servant!"

Day 16

Food for Thought

Thinking about rewards can expose familiar tensions between God's work and our participation. Will the giving of rewards lead to envy or boasting? In death, does the emphasis somehow shift to my own merit? In an interview for a Desiring God podcast, John Piper reminds us of a glorious truth about the concrete rewards which correspond to each believer's life of obedience: "We don't earn the rewards. They are graciously given by God. We don't deserve them. And they will be evidences that God looks with favor upon his own work of grace in our lives, working through us."[1] As such, all glory will be given to Christ! We will glory in Christ through rewards we receive and rewards we witness others receiving. There will be no room for envy or boasting in view of the glory due to Christ.

Faith in Action

Take some time to think about the gifts and resources that God has poured into your life. Then, reflect on how you're currently leveraging them for kingdom purposes. Who would you be in Jesus' parable? Would you be the servant who is investing in God's kingdom? Or, would you be the servant who currently has his talents "hidden in the ground?" 1 Corinthians 4:2 states, "It is required of stewards that they be found trustworthy." In other words, faithfulness to God's Kingdom work is an evidence of a wise and obedient manager. That's who and what God wants you to be. Does that describe you today?

Prayer

As you pray today, spend some time talking to God about your role as a manager in his kingdom. Be honest with him about your current investments. If necessary, confess the sin of negligence and commit to be more intentional about engaging in Kingdom work. Ask God to help you take the gifts and resources he has given you and use them for maximum impact in the kingdom through his church.

---

1. Piper, John [Interview]. January 30, 2017. "Will Some People in Heaven Have More Joy Than Others?" *Ask Pastor John*, Ep. 996. Desiringgod.org. Retrieved from https://www.desiringgod.org/interviews/will-some-people-in-heaven-have-more-joy-than-others

Day 17

Banquet Seats

Luke 14:1-11

Pride is our most dangerous enemy. It is the wraith that lurks in the shadows of our hearts, poisoning every motive and tainting every action. Pride says, "If you want to be fulfilled, it's up to you. If you want to be successful, it's up to you. If you want to be exalted, you've got to fight your way to the top by whatever means necessary. Then, you will be truly happy." Surprisingly, pride has its origins in the corridors of heaven. Lucifer, one of God's majestic archangels, was its first victim. In a moment of tragic self-awareness, he looked with envy at God's throne and said, "I will ascend to heaven... I will set my throne on high; I will sit on the mount of the assembly in the far reaches of the north; I will ascend above the heights of the clouds; I will make myself like the Most High (Is. 14:13-14)." God cast him out of heaven for his arrogant insolence, but he remained committed to his goal.

His first act of cosmic terrorism was perpetrated against Adam and Eve. When he tempted Eve to disobey God's command regarding the tree of the knowledge of good and evil, he used his own desires to bait her. He said, "God knows that when you eat of it your eyes will be opened, and you will be like God, knowing good and evil (Gen 3:5)." The desire to be a god is addicting—Eve quickly succumbed to its allure, and Adam was all too will-

Kingdom Fruits

> Humility allows us to rejoice with those who rejoice and to trust God's heart for us.

ing to follow her (Gen 3:6). In an instant, God's perfect creation was corrupted, and the human heart was infused with both the knowledge and presence of evil. Pride is now the root of every act of rebellion against God. It is at the core of every sin. And, it is an enemy of the gospel of grace, which says "I can't, but Jesus did."

In today's text, Jesus was attending a dinner party hosted by a big-shot Pharisee. When it was time to be seated for the meal, Jesus watched as the other people at the party tried to maneuver themselves into the positions closest to their host. After all, he had the power to improve the circumstances of their lives. If they could somehow capture his attention and be recognized, then the potential for social promotion increased exponentially.

Once everyone had taken their places, the bemused Jesus shared a parable about some people who attended a banquet (a little "on the nose," perhaps). He told the story of a man who, because of a gross miscalculation of his personal significance, chose a seat of honor close to the host. His climb to the top was halted abruptly when the host brought a friend over and gave him the man's seat. Then, the host asked the now displaced and disgraced guest to go sit in the worst seat at the banquet. Jesus ended the story by saying that the arrogant "climber" was filled with shame as the entire group witnessed his humiliation first hand—a humiliation resulting from the curse of pride.

Can you imagine the hush that filled the room when Jesus reached this point of the parable? I have to believe that Jesus was looking at the very people whom he had observed frantically trying to squeeze their way into the choice seats of honor. And, I have to believe that they were now shifting uncomfortably in those seats, averting their gaze and feeling the warmth of embarrassment on their faces.

Day 17

After pausing for dramatic effect, Jesus began to break down what the parable meant to help his listeners understand and apply it. He said, in essence, "The next time you go to a party, choose an insignificant place to sit. It will help you in two ways. First, if your host thinks you're a 'nobody,' and he wants you in an insignificant seat, you won't be embarrassed when he has to force you to move. This will spare you from forever being known as 'that person' who was humiliated at the party. Second, if your host thinks you're a 'somebody,' and he wants you in a seat of honor, he will move you, and you will be honored in front of everybody. Then, you'll be forever known as the person who got to sit in the great seats." Notice that seat selection is, ultimately, the job of the host. Where the guests choose to sit initially does not necessarily dictate where they sit eventually. Rather, their choice demonstrates how they see themselves and how they see the host. Choosing an insignificant seat conveys an understanding of the greater glory of the host and a deep trust in the host's ability to seat the guests.

Jesus concluded his parable with a bombshell: "For everyone who exalts himself will be humbled, and he who humbles himself will be exalted." In one brief sentence, Jesus ripped away his hearers' façades, exposing the prideful motives of their posturing. Remember what we know about this audience. Some Pharisees practiced their works before others, praying loudly, giving offerings only with an audience, comparing their religious performance to others, and vying to be counted among the most spiritual. They conflated external activity with internal transformation and were convinced of their spiritual superiority and deservedness. But, Jesus revealed that, in God's kingdom, it is the humble who will be exalted.

Humility recognizes our dependence on God to invite us and seat us at his table.

In the final section of our study, we are turning our attention to specific fruits that bear witness to our residency in God's kingdom.

Kingdom Fruits

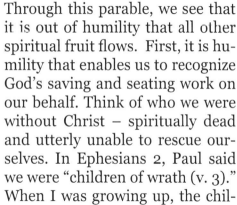

As we abide in humility, daily surrendering to the lordship of Christ, we will bear the fruit of obedience towards God and his word.

Through this parable, we see that it is out of humility that all other spiritual fruit flows. First, it is humility that enables us to recognize God's saving and seating work on our behalf. Think of who we were without Christ – spiritually dead and utterly unable to rescue ourselves. In Ephesians 2, Paul said we were "children of wrath (v. 3)." When I was growing up, the children had their own table at family gatherings. They didn't take the place of honor next to the Grandparents. Add to that identity the words "of wrath," and you don't have a recipe for the seat of honor at a banquet. That is who we were. We did not deserve a place of honor at the banquet any more than we deserved to be invited to the banquet in the first place. "But God, being rich in mercy, because of the great love with which he loved us...made us alive together with Christ (vv. 4-5)." Notice the imagery Paul used next: God "raised us up with him and *seated us* with him in the heavenly places in Christ Jesus (v. 6, emphasis mine)." Humility recognizes our dependence on God to invite us and seat us at his table.

Second, it is humility that drives us to abide in Christ. We know that we cannot produce spiritual fruit in our own strength. Only in a posture of humility can we give up illusions of our own spiritual greatness and cease our striving for seats of honor. In humility, we stop comparing our performance to others'. We see fruits of righteousness as gifts of grace flowing out of abiding in the vine of Christ's righteousness. As we abide in humility, daily surrendering to the lordship of Christ, we will bear the fruit of obedience towards God and his word.

It makes sense that humility, the foundational fruit of life in God's kingdom, would be the antithesis of pride, the fruit of death. Pride says, "I can." Pride tempts us to believe that we can justify ourselves according to our own standard. Pride teaches us that we can satisfy ourselves

Day 17

with all the world offers. Pride trusts that our wisdom, strength, and might will be enough to accomplish our plans for ourselves – and that our plans will mean something in the end. Those lies are the fruit of death eaten first in the Garden and consumed by every human since.

When God graciously rescues us, he teaches us the humility that says, "I can't." Humility says, "I cannot save myself, transform myself, satisfy myself, carry out cosmic plans, accomplish Kingdom purposes, or create meaning for myself." Only God can rescue, transform, satisfy, and work all of his purposes together for the good of his kingdom. This is the fruit of abundant life found and lived when all of our hope for life and death rests on the saving and transforming work of Christ in us.

Living in humility leads to great peace in this life. And, God's word reveals that humility also leads to honor in God's kingdom. Proverbs 15:33 says, "The fear of the Lord is instruction in wisdom, and humility comes before honor." Another proverb says "The reward for humility and fear of the Lord is riches and honor and life (Pr 22:4)." James describes the impact of humility on our relationship with God: "'God opposes the proud, and gives grace to the humble.' Resist the devil, and he will flee from you. Draw near to God, and he will draw near to you. . . . Humble yourselves before the Lord, and he will exalt you (James 4:6-10)." These scriptures give us a glimpse into how God delights in humility.

We may not know exactly what rewards and exaltation will look like in God's kingdom. Just like the host of the party, God is ultimately in charge of seat selection in this life and the next. On earth, he elevates some in his time and for his good purposes. Humility allows us to rejoice with those who rejoice and to trust God's heart for us. It allows us to depend on him in notoriety and in anonymity. In eternity, the glori-

Pride is now the root of every act of rebellion against God. It is at the core of every sin. And, it is an enemy of the gospel of grace, which says "I can't, but Jesus did."

Kingdom Fruits

Only God can rescue, transform, satisfy, and work all of his purposes together for the good of his kingdom.

ous reality is that God *has* seated us in the heavenly places through Christ – not because of any merit we possess, but "that in the coming ages he might show the immeasurable riches of his grace in kindness toward us in Christ Jesus (Eph 2:7)." This truth dismantles pride and keeps us running daily to the throne of grace.

Day 17

Food for Thought Read Philippians 2:1-18. Here, Paul gives us a glorious picture of God highly exalting a humility lived perfectly. Jesus, though in the form of God, emptied himself, "not counting equality with God a thing to be grasped (v. 6)." Notice the direct contrast to Satan's desires to be like the Most High and his lies in the Garden: "you will be like God!" Jesus, already God, takes on flesh and becomes obedient to a humiliating death so that we might become the children of God. If God exalts the humble, what is Jesus' reward for perfect humility? Paul tells us: "Therefore God has highly exalted him and bestowed on him the name that is above every name (v. 9)."

Faith in Action Jesus is perfect in humility; as a result, we can live humbly when we abide in him: "Have this mind among yourselves, which is yours in Christ Jesus (Phil 2:5)." Pride is dangerous to us because it hinders us from seeing our need to abide in Jesus, the source of our salvation and our righteousness. Spend some time identifying specific areas in your life in which you have taken the prideful posture of "I can." Consider ways in which you are looking to seat yourself in a position of honor. Instead, trust God to promote and tear down according to his good purposes. Examine ways in which you are trying to seat others, comparing religious performances and making judgments. Today, let the Holy Spirit examine your heart instead. Let him remind you of your need for mercy first, and rejoice in the gifts God has given you in Christ.

Prayer As you pray today, ask God the Holy Spirit to reveal areas of pride in your heart, and confess them as sin. This can be painful, but it will be profitable. Then, ask God to help you remember your utter dependence on him for life, salvation, and transformation.

Day 18

Two Foundations

Luke 6:46-49

It is incredibly difficult to follow directions. Tucked away deep inside each of us is a strong resistance towards authority figures. We want to be in control of our own lives and choices, so we rebel against those who are in positions to tell us what to do. How and when this rebellion manifests itself is unique to every individual, but generally it occurs at some point in the childhood years. It is that moment when a child is given an instruction by a parent, teacher, or coach, and for the first time, he consciously knows that he does not want to obey it. For the rest of his or her life, he will struggle with following instructions from parents, teachers, bosses, law enforcement personnel, pastors, and other authority figures.

As adults, the struggle to follow instructions can manifest itself in both harmless and harmful ways. For instance, my Dad regularly attempted to assemble things while the directions sat untouched on the floor. He would pick up a part, look at it intently while considering his task, and ask me this question: "I wonder where this goes?" Dad believed there was nothing so complex that it couldn't be solved on the basis of trial and error. Clearly, for many people, instructions are merely suggestions.

I carried Dad's approach to assembly projects into my adult years, too. Finally, I began to read the directions.

Kingdom Fruits

> *We don't like anyone telling us what to do, even if that someone is God.*

Yet because of my curious nature, I added a new twist to the "failure to follow instructions" process. I like to look at directions and try to find a better way to do it. Surely, I know more than the people who designed the product. Recently, I sought out some information from a master beekeeper about how to feed sugar water to my bee hives for the winter. She told me to cut the top off of some milk jugs, insert sticks and pine straw into the bottom half of the jug, and pour in the sugar water. Then, she told me to place them on the top of the beehives, surround them with an empty hive box, and put on the hive covers. She said the bees would do the rest.

As I was working on this project, I decided that her plan could be improved upon by first lining the milk jugs with porch screen. This would give the bees a ladder from which they could escape the sugar water from all angles. Finally, I assembled the jugs, added the sugar water, and placed them in the hives. Then, I waited for two days to see if the bees were gathering it. When I opened the hives, I discovered that all of it was already gone! I was preparing to add some more sugar water when I noticed that nearly 20 bees were trapped underneath the screen. It was then that I understood the foolishness of my plan—if I didn't remove the screen, the sugar water could drown all of the bees. In the end, I followed the master beekeeper's plan exactly. However, I wasted time, effort, and supplies by trying to make the instructions fit my own ill-conceived ideas.

In today's parable, Jesus addresses our propensity for ignoring directions. Jesus was teaching "a great multitude of people from all Judea and Jerusalem and the seacoast of Tyre and Sidon, who came to hear him and to be healed of their diseases (vv. 17-18)." During his message, Je-

> *Strong houses are always built on strong foundations.*

Day 18

While it is easy to say that Jesus is our Lord, it is harder to demonstrate that he is our Lord.

...sus commanded his followers to love their enemies, not to judge or condemn others, and to forgive others. He laid out specific instructions for what it looks like when we walk in humility before God and others.

He concluded his teaching with today's parable. He asked his followers, "Why do you call me 'Lord, Lord,' and not do what I tell you (v. 46)?" This is a profound question, and it digs down to the real issue behind our disobedience—we don't like anyone telling us what to do even if that someone is God. To underscore the seriousness of this question, Jesus told the parable of the two foundations. In it, he shared that there are two groups of people who call him "Lord": the wise and the foolish.

Jesus talked first about a wise builder. This builder had both a good plan and good materials for his construction project. Beyond this, he had a good premise for building: strong houses are always built on strong foundations. As a result, he dug deep into the ground until he hit rock, and he began laying his foundation there. Only when the foundation was correct did he begin to frame up the house. Later, tragedy struck. A massive storm dumped so much rain that the river overflowed its banks. A raging torrent of water washed through town, but his house endured the catastrophe because of its strong foundation.

Next, Jesus talked about a foolish builder. This builder also had a good plan and good materials for a construction project. Sadly, though, he had a flawed premise for building: strong houses may be built on any type of foundation. Whether it was ignorance or laziness, this builder chose to build his house on the surface of the ground. He built his house quickly, and from all appearances, it was beautiful in-

Obedience reveals authentic surrender to Jesus' Lordship.

Kingdom Fruits

> It's too late to build a strong foundation for our life through obedience to God's word when the river is spilling over its banks.

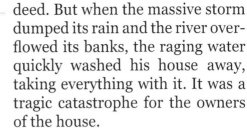

deed. But when the massive storm dumped its rain and the river overflowed its banks, the raging water quickly washed his house away, taking everything with it. It was a tragic catastrophe for the owners of the house.

Clearly, Jesus was talking about more than construction projects. He was using the wise and foolish builders to represent the two groups of people who call him "Lord." What makes them different? Jesus noted that wise people come to him, hear his word, and obey it. Because they have surrendered to him as their Lord, they are willing to obey his word. On the other hand, foolish people come to Jesus and hear his words, but they refuse to follow his instructions.

Remember, Jesus had just spent time describing the life of a follower. The crowd would be examining their lives in light of Jesus' commands to love, give, forgive, and show mercy. With his parable, he highlighted the significant implications of obedience. First, obedience reveals authentic surrender to Jesus' Lordship. While it is easy to say that Jesus is our Lord, it is harder to demonstrate that he is our Lord. We are prone to trust our own logic and emotions. We tend to build our lives – our priorities, decisions for the future, and our daily actions – on our own wisdom and ideals. We want to be lord. But, when we obey Jesus' commands, we demonstrate our surrender to his Lordship. Obeying his commands requires us to trust his wisdom. When Jesus is Lord, we build our lives on his priorities; we make plans that seek to further his kingdom; and, we walk in humble submission to his word in our daily actions.

The second implication Jesus revealed is that obedience affects our outcome in the storm. The house whose foundation rested on the rock withstood the flood that broke against it because, Jesus said, "it had been well built (v. 48)." To get to the solid foundation, the builder had to

Day 18

dig deeply. The imagery, here, is of hard work and commitment. We have seen in our study that following Jesus is costly and necessitates renouncing all. It counters our innate sinful desire to be masters of our own destiny and seekers of our own glory. Following Jesus as Lord is difficult. But, when we do, we join in God's work of building an unshakable house, an imperishable kingdom! When the storm hits, neither will we be shaken.

Those who say that Jesus is their Lord but fail to obey his word are like those who build a house without establishing a sure foundation. Trusting their wisdom, foresight, and plans, they call the shots. Rather than renouncing all to follow Jesus, they just keep an eye on those around them to make sure they're performing well enough to blend in and get by. The great tragedy is that their foundation is illusory. When the storm hits, the house will fall, and the ruin will be great.

The question for us today is simple: Am I obeying Jesus' commands, or am I living in disobedience? The answer to this question is important because today could be the day when the storm hits. It's too late to build a strong foundation for our life through obedience to God's word when the river is spilling over its banks. We must begin this process today.

Kingdom Fruits

Food for Thought

Jesus asked, "Why call me Lord and not do what I tell you?" Read Jesus' whole sermon in Luke 6:17-7:1 and identify the commands he made. Consider underlining, highlighting, or making a list in your journal. Then, think about yesterday's study on humility. In what ways is humility necessary in order to follow each of Jesus' commands? This side of his resurrection, we have access to the power of the Holy Spirit to enable us to obey. Rejoice again in the wonderful grace of Jesus, and abide in him today.

Faith in Action

What areas of your life are you struggling to submit to the Lordship of Christ? Is it a sinful relationship, a secret addiction, a consistent sin, a persistent doubt, a crippling fear, or maybe something else? Today, spend time thinking about that area of your life. What would change in your life if you submitted it to the Lordship of Christ? If your struggle is too deep, make plans to talk with your pastor about finding a good Christian counselor to help you.

Prayer

As you pray today, pause to confess any areas of your life that you've been refusing to submit to the Lordship of Christ. Ask God to give you the strength to surrender that area of your life to him today and to make choices in that area that reflect obedience.

Two Sons

Matthew 21:28-32

Life is filled with epiphanies—the "Aha" moments that shape our understanding of the world. I remember vividly the first time I touched a hot stove as a toddler. In that moment of searing pain (literally) I had an epiphany: touching things that are hot is a foolish decision. Similarly, I remember the first time I decided to ride a bike downhill, training wheels and all. The emotions are etched in my mind: exhilaration, followed by concern, and ending in panic. That brief downhill ride ended abruptly at the rear end of my Dad's car. I had another epiphany: brakes are an important component on a bike and should be utilized often.

As we age, we experience more profound epiphanies. When we find ourselves in difficult circumstances, we may have this epiphany: real friends are hard to find, so when you find one, you better hang on to them. Upon the birth of a child, we have yet another epiphany: children are miraculous gifts from God. And when someone close to us dies, we have perhaps the most profound epiphany of all: life is precious and must be lived with intentionality.

Today's parable provides us with an opportunity to have an "Aha" moment in our spiritual lives. In fact, it reveals to us one of the most important spiritual truths we will ever learn. In today's text, Jesus is talking once again

Kingdom Fruits

In Christ...we have an unmistakable purpose on this earth.

with a group of religious and political leaders in Israel. They were observing and questioning Jesus, because they were looking for reasons to arrest him. Ultimately, they wanted to eliminate him as a threat to their power base (Mt 21:45-46).

As Jesus talked with them, he told them a parable about a dad who had two sons. As is the case in many homes, the two sons had very different personalities. The first son was regularly unconcerned about his dad's thoughts or plans for him. As a result, he was rebellious; he was the classic problem child. The second son was the compliant one. He was regularly obedient and quick to respond to his father's requests. He was the favored child in the family.

One day, the father went to the first son and told him to go work in the family vineyard. His answer was a short and predictable, "I will not." He wasn't interested in working hard in the vineyard. He had his own plans for the day. So, the father sought out his second son and gave him the same command. He answered a swift and respectful, "I go, sir." I'm sure his father was overwhelmed again by his favorite son's obedience, even as his frustration with his rebellious child grew stronger by the moment. Leaving his sons, he turned his attention to managing his business.

Had Jesus ended the story here, we would all be very comfortable. After all, this is a classic example with which we're all somewhat familiar. Many of us would see ourselves in the good son, while looking down on the rebellious sibling we all can picture in our minds. But, there is a huge plot twist in the story. For reasons unknown, the rebellious son had a change of heart. Rather than ignore his father for the umpteenth time, he chose to obey. Despite his initial response, he went to work in the family vineyard. I can imagine his father's surprise later that day when he discovered his son working in the vineyard.

Day 19

Similarly, the compliant son had a change of heart as well. Rather than go to work in the vineyard, he chose to disobey has father and stay home. He didn't seem to care if he broke his word. I imagine his decision was equally baffling to his father.

Now that everyone listening to the story was confused, Jesus provided them with the explanation. He told them that the rebellious son represented the worst of people in Jewish society—the tax collectors and prostitutes. They were the outcasts, living in rebellion against God and his word. Yet, when they heard John the Baptist teaching about the way of righteousness, they had a change of heart. They believed John, and they began to obey God with their lives. The compliant son, Jesus said, represented the Pharisees and other religious leaders in Jewish society. Even though they had heard John the Baptist, and seen the transformation in the lives of the tax collectors and prostitutes, they refused to believe him. As a result, they had not experienced a change of heart. They obeyed the law, but they did it for all of the wrong reasons.

As he sometimes did, Jesus was operating on two planes in this parable. In the first, Jesus explained a significant implication of his ministry: both Jews and Gentiles, men and women, and poor and rich would enjoy fellowship with God through the priestly mediation of Christ. Jesus came to fulfill the Old Testament law, instituting a new covenant through his blood. This new covenant would not require yearly, location-based sacrifice to atone for sins; instead, Jesus made a once-for-all sacrifice on the cross (Heb 10:10-14). His resurrection proved that God accepted his sacrifice on behalf of all who believe in his finished work and confess that he is Lord. Therefore, those who were once outside of the Old Testament covenant could be welcomed into God's kingdom. In fact, Jesus taught that those who once were far off enter God's kingdom with greater ease because

Every person who is a Kingdom resident has both a role and a responsibility within God's kingdom.

Kingdom Fruits

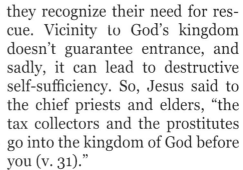

> We can serve our Father with joy and in total rest, trusting that he will fulfill his purposes through us.

they recognize their need for rescue. Vicinity to God's kingdom doesn't guarantee entrance, and sadly, it can lead to destructive self-sufficiency. So, Jesus said to the chief priests and elders, "the tax collectors and the prostitutes go into the kingdom of God before you (v. 31)."

In the second plane of this parable, we can apply Jesus' teaching to our understanding of what our lives will look like when we are walking in obedience. On this plane, we see God's will for us as members in his kingdom. The father said to his sons, "Go and work in the vineyard today (v. 28)." God's will for us as Kingdom residents is to obey that very same call. The vineyard represents God's kingdom on earth, and every person who is a Kingdom resident has both a role and a responsibility within it. As we saw in the parable of the talents, we are not merely Kingdom receivers but Kingdom managers. We are called to be faithful managers of the gifts and resources God gives to us. Fulfilling that role requires Spirit-empowered obedience to our mission.

When believers fail to pursue the mission of God's kingdom, one of two things may be happening. First, we may be ignorant – or forgetful – of God's will for us in this life. How quick we are to forge our own path and begin to follow our own aims. Look around, and you will see people turning their heads wildly in pursuit of purpose – in jobs, in relationships, in new hobbies or trends. Loss or failure in those pursuits leads to despair and a new search. In Christ, however, we have an unmistakable purpose on this earth. Jesus' parting words called us to go and make disciples. He sent the Holy Spirit to empower believers to accomplish this mission, and he promised to be with them always. Then, in 1 Corinthians 12, the apostle Paul described specific resources given to Kingdom residents to use for the building up of the body. Wisdom, knowledge, faith, discernment – these gifts are empowered by God,

Day 19

given "for the common good (v. 7)" of the body, and apportioned to "each one individually as [God] wills (v. 11)." God intends for us to use our God-given, Spirit-empowered gifts to advance his kingdom. Remembering our purpose and obeying his call to work in the vineyard leads to great joy and deep peace.

Second, believers may fail to obey God's call when we intend to obey God's will... someday. In this case, we understand and appreciate that God has given us an eternal purpose on earth. We may even celebrate that we get to be part of his kingdom and look forward to the day when we might participate in the work that he is doing around us. We are masters at convincing ourselves that today is not the day to work in the vineyard: If we can just save a little more money, we will be ready to start giving generously. Once we make it through the next semester, our schedule will open up for more ministry opportunities. After our kids go to college, we'll really be ready to serve the community better. Perhaps, if we could just get a little more training, we would be ready to do a great job. We are sure someone else is far better suited for that role at this time.

This can be a dangerous space to occupy because we begin to believe that intention is the same as action. If you've ever had someone say to you, "Oh, I meant to (give you a call, do the dishes, fill up your gas tank)," you understand that intentions do not get the job done. In today's parable, Jesus asked his hearers, "which of the two sons did the will of the father (v. 31)." Their answer was correct: the son who, though he rejected the command at first, "changed his mind and went (v. 29)." The son who said, "Yes, yes, of course I'll go," but didn't actually go work in the vineyard was clearly not doing the will of the father. Remember Jesus' words yesterday: "Why do you call me 'Lord, Lord' and not do what I tell you (Lk 6:46)?"

God intends for us to use our God-given, Spirit-empowered gifts to advance his kingdom.

Kingdom Fruits

Doing the will of our Father means leveraging our gifts to make disciples and encourage the body. Today, Jesus wants you to have a spiritual epiphany moment—as a resident in his kingdom, you are given a glorious and fulfilling purpose on earth. You are tasked with a mission: "Go and work in the vineyard today." Over the course of our study, we have seen that our work is for God's glory, not our own; through Christ's righteousness, not our own; and in the Spirit's power, not our own. As a result, we can serve our Father with joy and in total rest, trusting that he will fulfill *his* purposes through us.

Day 19

Food for Thought

Read Psalm 138. Pay attention to the psalmist's description of the power of God and the work that he accomplishes on earth. By contrast, how does the psalmist describe himself and his power? As you reflect on specific ways to leverage your gifts and resources for God's kingdom, remember the Source of our salvation, our gifting, all we possess, our very lives. My hope is not that I will work enough to fulfill God's purposes for him; my hope is that "God will fulfill his purpose for me (Ps 138:8)."

Faith in Action

Have you identified your Spirit-given areas of giftedness? Have you begun to work in God's kingdom through your church? If so, how does remembering your eternal purpose increase your excitement and passion to labor on? If you're not currently serving God through your local church, contact your pastor today and discuss the ministry opportunities that currently exist in your church.

Prayer

Talk with God today about his command to work in his kingdom. Be honest with him about your obedience in ministry. Practice confession where necessary and commit your heart to "go work in the vineyard today."

Day 20

Dishonest Manager

Luke 16:1-13

In today's text, Jesus told one of his most curious parables. It's the story of a company manager who was embezzling money from his employer. This is a classic case of "the more things change the more they stay the same." Embezzling remains a huge problem in our world today. In America alone, it's estimated that 50 million dollars are embezzled from companies every year.[1] Most of the time, employees steal money from their employers to fix an immediate financial crisis in their lives. However, after they've taken money once, it becomes easier to do so again. Soon, they develop a lifestyle of stealing. Ultimately, most are fired and prosecuted for their crimes.

In this story, Jesus introduces us to the manager—a man who was "wasting" the owner's "possessions." In other words, he was misappropriating the owner's money for his own personal use. When the owner finally discovered it, he called the man in and fired him on the spot. That's when the story gets interesting. Immediately, the newly unemployed manager began to strategize for his future. Because he was in management, he was ill-equipped for many jobs. The text mentions two: ditch-digging and begging. It's interesting that he would consider these two, random

---

1. Pofeldt, Elaine. (2017). "This crime in the workplace is costing US businesses $50 billion a year." *CNBC*.

Kingdom Fruits

...worship exists in our daily affections.

professions. The first was hard manual labor (he was too soft for this work), while the second was easy but would require throwing himself upon the mercy of others (he was too proud for this work). Evidently, nothing else entered his mind as an option. He knew how to be a manager—nothing else. Unfortunately, he was a dishonest manager, so re-entering that field was going to be tough.

He may have been dishonest, but the text states that he was "shrewd." In other words, he was a thief, but he wasn't a dumb thief—it takes savvy to embezzle money for a long time without getting caught. So, he launched an ingenious scheme. He knew that if the word got out that he was a thief, he would never find another cushy, management gig. Quickly, he conceived of a plan that would foster goodwill with many of the business owners and community leaders who owed his boss money.

One by one, the shrewd manager called the business men and women into his boss' commodities brokerage and began to wheel-and-deal. One owed 900 gallons of oil, and the shrewd manager allowed him to settle his debt at the price of 450 gallons of oil—what a bargain. Another owed 1,000 bushels of wheat, and the shrewd manager allowed her to settle for the price of 800 bushels of wheat—another fantastic savings. One by one, he made these incredible deals available. In this way, he reduced his boss' debts (below market value of course), while making all of his potential, future employers happy and pleased with his work. Ultimately, the dishonest manager's plan worked perfectly. He may have lost his job, but he gained a ton of new friends, who now "owed" him for their amazing business deals. I'm sure he landed another job in management, and probably embezzled from them too.

As you might imagine, his plan placed his boss in a bind from which he could not escape. On the one hand, he was receiving money on debts owed. While this was good,

Day 20

he wasn't receiving the full amount owed, and so his profit wasn't as strong as he wanted. On the other hand, the now fired manager was communicating to the boss' customers that this was the boss' idea. They were so thankful to him, and he was getting so much community affirmation, he couldn't cancel the deep discounts—he had to honor them. His reputation went up, but his profits went down. And, I'm sure, he never saw any of the money that the dishonest manager stole from him. All he could do was shake his head in amazement. He'd been outwitted by his manager once again. The text states, "The master commended the dishonest manager for his shrewdness."

Of course, Jesus wasn't affirming the dishonest manager's sins of greed, coveting, and stealing. The fictional business owner in the story, who had been hood-winked twice by his manager, was the one offering begrudging praise for his manager's schemes. The scriptures make it clear that greed, coveting, and stealing are sinful actions which Christians should avoid at all costs (Ex 20:15, 17; Lk 12:15, Eph 4:28). Jesus was not encouraging his listeners to become more shrewd at earthly business pursuits; instead, he was commanding them to pursue something else entirely.

Jesus had a lot to say about money because he knew that the love of money is a primary temptation for the human heart. Why? The Swiss Reformer John Calvin once explained that the human heart is a factory for creating idols, or unworthy recipients of our worship. When we think about worship, we may think first of congregational singing on Sundays, but worship exists in our daily affections – what we think about for happiness, what we focus on for purpose, what we glory in for meaning, what we trust in for security, what we hope in for joy. Our affections are always flowing out toward something or someone. God is the only one worthy to receive our love, yet our affections

"True riches" are the lasting treasures in heaven that we possess in Christ.

Kingdom Fruits

> How we use our money reveals our affections.

are prone to wander. We are factories for churning out lesser gods whom we imagine will provide, fulfill, and deliver.

Money is an easy target for our worship because many of the lesser gods we look to depend on money. Financial security requires just a little more money in the savings account. To maintain our sense of value, we pour money into beauty products and gym memberships. If we could just take that vacation with our friends, buy a bigger house, purchase our kids that thing they want, or afford that procedure, we would finally be happy. Money fuels the idol factory. Jesus confirmed, "You cannot serve God and money (v. 13)."

What, then, should our relationship with money be? In this parable, Jesus provides some building blocks for how Kingdom residents should think about money. First, he reminds us that there are two currency categories: "unrighteous wealth (v. 9)" and "true riches (v. 11)." The phrase "unrighteous wealth" is used to describe money that can be earned and spent on earth. It is often the measure of success in this world and, as a result, "the sons of this world (v. 8)" focus their efforts on making and keeping this money. The dishonest manager was so fixated on money that he was willing to act illegally to obtain it. Then, when he was caught, he was willing to harm his boss – the source of his initial wealth– in order to maintain it. The sad reality for those chasing unrighteous wealth is that it doesn't last. In his Sermon on the Mount, Jesus said, "Do not lay up for yourselves treasures on earth, where moth and rust destroy and where thieves break in and steal (Mt 6:19)." The worth of earth's currency is constantly in flux; it can be stolen; it can be squandered. Most importantly, it will mean nothing when our souls depart from this world. On the other hand, "true riches" are the lasting treasures in heaven that we possess in Christ. As we saw in the parable of the Hidden Treasures, Jesus saves us to an eternal

Day 20

inheritance. Our riches in him are true. They are imperishable. For those of us who are in Christ, that knowledge is cause for rejoicing.

Second, Jesus revealed that how we spend our unrighteous wealth affects how we experience true riches. He warned his listeners to consider carefully how to utilize their money because "when it fails (v. 9)," it will matter how they had invested it. Here, he separates the use of earthly money into two categories: faithful and unfaithful.

When we use our unrighteous wealth faithfully, we use our financial resources for the good of God's kingdom. Scripture reveals that monetary giving begins with the tithe: 10% of our gross income (and everything else that we have), belongs to God. He commands us to give it so that his kingdom will have the financial resources necessary to carry the gospel to the ends of the earth (Mal 3:6-12). Jesus himself affirmed the tithe when he said, "Render to Caesar the things that are Caesar's [pay your taxes], and to God the things that are God's [pay your tithes and offerings] (Mt 22:21, emphasis mine)." Jesus never revoked the tithe—instead he affirmed it. Further, the scriptures command us to give generously from the 90% that God allows us to manage (2 Cor 9:6-15). These are freewill offerings given to Kingdom endeavors. Often, this looks like generously giving to others in need. In fact, Jesus said that when we give time and money to God's kingdom, we "make friends for ourselves (v.9)." Those friends who benefit from our spiritual investment will be the ones waiting to "receive [us] into the eternal dwellings (v. 9)." What a reward! This is what it looks like to "lay up for yourselves treasures in heaven, where neither moth nor rust destroys and where thieves do not break in and steal (Mt 6:19-20)."

When we use our earthly wealth unfaithfully, we hoard it and selfishly consume it. The temptation is to believe that us-

When our worship is misplaced, we are cut off from the abiding vine of Christ and are, therefore, incapable of bearing fruit and pursuing God's will for our lives.

ing our unrighteous wealth unfaithfully is not that big of a deal: *"So, we won't make friends for ourselves to welcome us into heaven. I don't need a gameday tunnel. And, okay, maybe my pursuits on earth won't last, but I'll sure enjoy them while I'm here! Heaven will still be awesome even if I don't have many treasures up there. That's not really what giving is supposed to be about anyway, right?"* It's easy to rationalize unfaithful management, but Jesus wanted us to understand the grave significance of how we use the money he entrusts us with on earth.

He said, "One who is faithful in a very little is also faithful in much, and one who is dishonest in a very little is also dishonest in much. If then you have not been faithful in the unrighteous wealth, who will entrust to you the true riches? (vv. 10-11)." This question is sobering because it gets to the very heart of our relationship with money. How we use our money reveals our affections. When we use our unrighteous wealth unfaithfully, we do not merely waste our energy on destructible pursuits. We do not merely arrive in heaven with fewer friends and money bags. We reveal that our affections are misplaced. Misplaced affections could mean that we have never understood the true riches of Christ and entered a saving relationship with Jesus. We use our money how we choose because we really don't believe that it will matter in the end.

If we are a resident of God's kingdom, we know that our eternal future is secure. We have been entrusted the true riches of Christ. To experience them in this life, though, we must abide in him. If our affections are misplaced, as a Kingdom resident, it means that we have lost sight of our true Treasure. Jesus said that it is impossible for a servant to serve two masters, "for either he will hate the one and love the other, or he will be devoted to the one and despise the other. You cannot serve God and money (v. 13)." When our worship is misplaced, we are cut off from the abiding vine of Christ and are, therefore, incapable of bearing fruit and pursuing God's will for our lives.

That is not where God wants us to be. He wants us to abide in Jesus, to bear fruit, and to pursue his purposes

Day 20

for our lives. He is infinitely worthy of our worship and the only one who can deliver on his promises to provide eternal purpose, unbreachable security, and lasting joy.

Kingdom Fruits

Food for Thought A popular false doctrine asserts that the more money you give, the more God will be compelled to bless you financially. Today, we call this false teaching, the "Prosperity Gospel," but this is not a new scheme. Read 1 Timothy 6:2-21, and note how Paul discredits the Prosperity Gospel. Consider what these verses reveal about earthly money (vv. 7-10, 17-19) and true riches (vv. 12, 19-20). Then, read aloud how Paul describes the source of our true Treasure – "he who is the blessed and only Sovereign, the King of kings and Lord of lords, who alone has immortality, who dwells in unapproachable light, whom no one has ever seen or can see. To him be honor and eternal dominion. Amen (vv. 15-16)."

Faith in Action Spend some time today evaluating your use of earthly money: what does it reveal about your heart's affections? Whom or what are you trusting in to provide, satisfy, and deliver? God is the only one who can provide us with life, resources, purpose, and eternal joy in fellowship with him and other believers. He is infinitely worthy of our worship. When we fix our affections on him, we can relinquish our hold on money and begin using it obediently and generously in God's kingdom.

Prayer If you are struggling with wandering affections today, ask God to help you to trust his promises to provide, satisfy, and deliver. Ask him for a greater understanding of the riches of his glorious grace that are your inheritance in Christ. Commit your earthly money to him – again or for the first time – and ask the Holy Spirit to empower your obedience and grow your generosity.

Day 21

Early and Late Workers Part One

Matthew 20:1-16

It was Shakespeare, while writing the tragedy *Othello*, who first referred to jealousy as the "green-eyed monster." Jealousy is resentment against the success or achievement of a peer or rival. Let's be honest—all of us know what it's like to be jealous of someone else: the football player who dates the prettiest cheerleader; the popular girl who becomes the Homecoming Queen; the student who receives the Fellowship with its full-ride scholarship; the woman who has the "perfect" job, husband, and family; the colleague who is named Salesman of the Year. Jealousy doesn't discriminate—it affects us all.

By the end of today's parable, jealousy will become a major player. But I'm getting ahead of myself. Once again, Jesus begins to talk about the kingdom of heaven. Remember, he began his ministry by declaring that the kingdom of God had arrived on earth. He could make this declaration, because Jesus is the King of the kingdom. Most of his teaching ministry is spent describing how we gain entrance to the kingdom and how our lives are transformed as King-

Kingdom Fruits

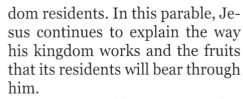

> When we see the achievements and blessings of others, we're often tempted to think poorly of God.

dom residents. In this parable, Jesus continues to explain the way his kingdom works and the fruits that its residents will bear through him.

Jesus told the story of a businessman who owned a vineyard. I suppose it was time for the harvest, and like many people both then and now, he needed to hire some day-laborers to work in his fields. He went and hired some men to work early in the morning. To fully understand this story, we have to first remind ourselves about the way they measured time in the first century. Without the benefit of modern clocks, which measure time down to the second, people measured time by daylight and dark—both of which consisted of approximately 12 hours. The first hour of the day, then, would have been the hour of sunrise. It appears that the vineyard owner hired his first workers around 6 am and promised to pay them one denarius—the common wage for 12 hours of work.

However, the businessman soon discovered that he needed more workers than he had hired, so he headed back into town to find other people who were waiting for work. At the third hour, or around 9 am, he sent them out into his fields as well. His promise for their payment was more vague. He said he would pay them "whatever is right" at the end of the day. Everyone would have known that this meant being paid for the amount of hours they worked. Throughout the day, the vineyard owner added to his workforce. He sent more workers out at the 6th hour (noon), and the 9th hour (3 pm) as well, promising to pay them what was right. Finally, as the day neared its end, he saw some more laborers still waiting in the square, hopeful for work even at the end of the day. The business man asked them a question: "Why do you stand here idle all day?" Their response was honest and simple: "Because no one has hired us." Realizing he could leverage their labor to squeeze some more profit out of the remaining daylight,

Day 21

he hurried them out to his vineyard to work at the 11th hour (5 pm).

One short hour later, daylight turned to dark, and the vineyard owner told his foreman to pay the workers and send them home. He gave the foreman an interesting process to follow. Rather than beginning with those whom he had hired first, he instructed the foreman to pay the workers in the reverse order they were hired. You can imagine their surprise when those hired at the 5 pm received a full denarius for one hour's work! Go ahead, put yourself in their shoes for a minute. What an amazing thing the business man did for them. He hired them to work for an hour, and they got paid for the full day! Don't you think you would have been amazed and grateful to receive that same payment?

Next, the foreman began to pay the 3 pm workers—they, too, got a full day's wage. They were followed by the noon and 9 am workers—they, too, got a full day's wage. Finally, the foreman called up the first group of workers who were hired at 6 am. I'm sure they were surprised to see the other workers being paid a full day's wage after working for only part of the day. But, their anticipation began to grow as they watched the process unfold. Surely they would receive a bonus for working the entire 12 hours. You can imagine their frustration when they, like those who came before them, received a single denarius for their work. Go ahead—pretend that you're one of those workers. How would you have responded? What would you have felt? I imagine it may have been similar to the way they felt: "And on receiving it they grumbled at the master of the house, saying, 'These last worked only one hour, and you have made them equal to us who have borne the burden of the day and the scorching heat (vv. 11- 12).'"

God's grace is the source of all blessings and benefits—not talent, effort, or achievement.

Notice the contrast between these groups of workers. Those who came later in the day

Kingdom Fruits

> *In God's kingdom, the weak are strong, the great are servants, the blessed give rather than receive, those who lose their lives find them, and those who are hired late in the day receive the same pay as those who have labored for hours.*

and received a full day's wages were ecstatic. However, those who worked for the entire day and received the same payment were angry and frustrated. Jealousy is conceived and birthed when we believe that we've been passed over for something we deserve. Normally, jealousy is preceded by one of two thoughts. First, jealousy asks, "Why don't I have that?" If we're honest, we'll admit that we ask this question routinely. Why don't I have his hair, her friends, their house, his position, her creativity, and the list goes on. There are a million ways we often think these thoughts, but each of them reveals an area of discontentment in our hearts. Second, jealousy asks, "Why doesn't God do that for me?" When we see the achievements and blessings of others, we're often tempted to think poorly of God. If God can bless others in a particular way that we covet, why can't he do the same for us? This form of discontentment turns our frustration from the particular situation to God himself. We know that God is sovereign over his world and our lives. If he hasn't given us something that we believe we've either earned or deserve, then we blame God. Jealousy does not just reveal a lack of contentment in our circumstances; it reveals a lack of contentment in God.

If you were reading today's parable carefully, you've already noticed how the early workers' response to their wages gives evidence of this. They were told by the vineyard owner that he would pay them one denarius for work that day. This was the daily wage amount, and they agreed to work for it. They may have been surprised to see the influx of workers throughout the day, but they imagined everyone would be paid for their hours worked—not a penny more. They were content in their work because of this. But, they were very surprised to see that every

144

Day 21

worker was receiving a full day's wage, even if they hadn't worked for the entire day. The final surprise was the reality that they were not going to receive more money. They were jealous that the other workers would receive the same pay for less work, while they had worked the longest and hardest. When the reality of the situation began to sink in, they grumbled against the vineyard owner. I'm guessing it went something like this: "Can you believe this guy? We've been here working all day in this stinking heat, and those jokers came in the last few hours and got the same amount of money as us? No sir... the owner of this vineyard is a jerk." Despite the fact that the vineyard owner paid them the agreed upon amount for their day's labor, they chose to blame him for being generous—more on that tomorrow.

Again and again, Jesus' message of the kingdom turns everything in the world upside down. In God's kingdom, the weak are strong, the great are servants, the blessed give rather than receive, those who lose their lives find them, and those who are hired late in the day receive the same pay as those who have labored for hours. As we study how we are called to live as Kingdom residents, today's parable reminds us that God's grace is the source of all blessings and benefit—not talent, effort, or achievement. The Bible says that God is the giver of all good gifts (James 1:17), and we must trust and rest in his sovereign purpose for our lives and the lives of those around us.

Kingdom Fruits

Food for Thought Both in our salvation and in his tangible blessings to us here on earth, we are undeserving recipients of God's grace. He has been generous to us in every way through Christ. To avoid discontented and jealous attitudes, we should learn to be content and to practice gratitude for God's provision. Tomorrow, we will examine specific ways to do that. Today, read Philippians 4:10-13. Pay special attention to the different circumstances that Paul mentions—some are great; some are awful. Yet, Paul learned to be content regardless.

Faith in Action Jealousy is so common in the human experience that you may be used to its presence. Observe your own heart carefully today to catch tugs of jealousy. Try to identify moments when you feel discontent. We are quick to distract ourselves from critical self-reflection, but paying attention to our thoughts and attitudes is one way that the Holy Spirit can convict us of sin. Should he do so today, confess and ask God to give you joy in all he has provided for you in Jesus.

Prayer Praise God for his good gifts in your life. Start with your salvation and the spiritual and eternal gifts that came with it. Then, thank God for the innumerable blessings in your life. Next, ask God to help you learn to be confident and joyful in his eternal provision in any earthly circumstance. Finally, feel free to ask God to meet your needs and grant the desires of your heart. God delights in his children, loves to hear our prayers, and is faithful to respond with all-surpassing peace (Phil 4:4-7).

Early and Late Workers Part Two

Matthew 20:1-16

"That's not fair!" The words hung like smoke in the air as my youngest daughter Cassie stared at me defiantly. "Why does she get to go?!" The silence that followed conjured a memory from long ago. In that memory, I was the defiant teenager asking the exact same thing of my father. His simple response would become a common refrain in my adult life, and I quietly repeated it to Cassie. "Life's not fair." In that moment, Cassie was frustrated and jealous that her sister Cherie, who was nearly three years older, was getting to go on an outing from which she was excluded. In her mind, she was perfectly capable of participating as well, but in the minds of her mother and me, she was not. Hence the common, human refrain—"That's not fair."

Yesterday, we began the study of a convicting parable of Jesus. As you remember, the workers who logged 12 hours in the vineyard were less than pleased that they were paid the same amount as those who had worked for an hour. Ultimately, they questioned the fairness of the

Kingdom Fruits

Comparison is a sure pathway to jealousy and discontentment.

vineyard owner in his distribution of payments. When the businessman heard that some of the workers were grumbling about him, he responded, "Friend, I am doing you no wrong. Did you not agree with me for a denarius? Take what belongs to you and go (vv. 13-14a)." As you can see, the workers' grumbling was unfounded, as was their claim that the businessman was unfair. When he hired them, they had all mutually agreed that he would pay them a denarius for the day—the common daily wage. They were more than happy to go to work for that price. As you remember, the problem arose when the vineyard owner chose to pay the subsequent people he hired the same amount for fewer hours worked.

The vineyard owner continued, "I choose to give to this last worker as I give to you. Am I not allowed to do what I choose with what belongs to me? Or do you begrudge my generosity? So the last will be first, and the first last (vv. 14b-16)." Here, the vineyard owner reminds his early laborers of some important truths. First, he had been gracious to hire them to work for the day. Without his willingness to hire them, they may have been unable to afford food that day. Second, he had been faithful to his word. He paid them exactly what he said he would pay them. Third, he had been wise and gracious in hiring additional workers throughout the day. The profits from the harvest provided the money for their wages. Fourth, he had been generous with the money God had given to him. He paid everyone the same thing—one day's wage—regardless of the amount of time they actually worked. Finally, the businessman owned the land, the vineyard, and the harvest. As a result, the money that it produced was his, and he could use it as he saw fit. Far from

In his complete power, God is free to distribute his money the way he wants.

Day 22

being unfair, all of these choices pointed to the gracious generosity of the vineyard owner.

Again, Jesus is teaching across several planes to reveal truths about the way that God works in his kingdom. First, Jesus is speaking about the relationship between the Jews and the Gentiles. The gospel of forgiveness through faith originated with Israel, but through the years they had begun to place more emphasis on their own works than God's grace. When Jesus came proclaiming the message of the kingdom, he told those in Israel that the original promise to Abraham included hope for the Gentile (Gen 12:3). This offended the Jews—after all, they came first. Yet, Jesus was willing to invite Gentiles to experience the forgiveness of sins through faith also. They were "late" to be included in God's redemptive plans, yet they were "first" to receive Jesus as their Messiah and Savior. Thus, Jesus ended this parable with these words: "So the last will be first, and the first last (v. 16)."

Second, Jesus highlights that comparison is a sure pathway to jealousy and discontentment. In light of the vineyard owner's kindness to the other laborers, the early workers became angry. Because they were hired first and worked the longest, they felt that they deserved to be paid more than the agreed-upon wage. As a result, they were not able to appreciate or enjoy the promised provision they received. Likewise, when God seems to be blessing someone else financially, it is easy for us to begin comparing their spiritual performance with our own. Perhaps we consider the length of time that they have been following Jesus or the speed and strength with which we perceive them to be serving God. When we put ourselves in the seat of judgment, we usually judge ourselves to be more deserving than others of God's favor, and we look with jealousy at their blessings and with discontentment at our own. As a result, we rob ourselves of experiencing the joy of God's presence and his promised provision.

By grace, God chose us in Christ to become Kingdom residents through faith.

149

Kingdom Fruits

> We find contentment when we cease to look around at what others have, and we remember to look up at what is ours in Christ.

Third, Jesus reveals that it is remembering the power and character of God which moves our hearts to contentment in him. In response to the early workers' attitudes, the vineyard owner asked, "Am I not allowed to do what I choose with what belongs to me? Or do you begrudge my generosity (v. 15)?" God is the owner of all things. In his complete power, God is free to distribute his money the way he wants, and he does so as an act of grace and generosity, in accordance with his will. Trusting in God's sovereign power enables us to consider the resources he has given us to be right and good and to focus on being good stewards for kingdom investment.

When we look jealously on how he blesses others, we resent the kind and generous character of which we also are undeserving recipients. Like the vineyard owner, God graciously chooses workers to participate in the kingdom of his Son. None of the laborers deserved to be chosen – the vineyard owner could have chosen others or no one. In the same way, none of us deserves to be recipients of the Kingdom. Our sin has earned for us only death (Rom 6:23). Yet, by grace, God chose us in Christ to become Kingdom residents through faith (Eph 1:4). As residents, each of us receives the same gifts of his generosity: forgiveness of sins, the covering of Christ's righteousness, adoption into God's family, the filling and sealing of God's Spirit, gifting through God's Spirit to labor in the kingdom, the supplying of our earthly needs, and an eternal home with God. Talk about amazing grace! Remembering God's gracious character enables us to trust that "God will supply every need" we have "according to his riches in glory in Christ Jesus (Phil 4:19)." We find contentment when we cease to look around at what others have, and we remember to look up at what is ours in Christ.

Day 22

Food for Thought Contentment is a spiritual fruit that gives evidence to our residency in God's kingdom. Like all other fruits of righteousness, it comes from abiding in Christ. Read Luke's account of the temptations of Jesus in chapter 4:1-13. Notice how each of Satan's temptations addresses a lack he imagined Jesus to have: food, power, help with sustaining his physical life. Reflect on Jesus' rebuffing of each temptation. How does he demonstrate unwavering trust in God's provision and plans for him? If you are tempted to fixate on a perceived lack in your life today, look to Jesus, instead. He is the source of our faith, our hope, and our future. He is for us (Ps 56), and he is with us (Mt 28:20).

Faith in Action When we struggle with jealousy and discontentment, we have lost sight of the riches of God's unmerited grace toward us and the value of our eternal inheritance in Christ. Reflect on your attitudes today. Are you in the habit of comparing your tangible blessings with that of others? Doing so is a recipe for jealousy. Do you measure your religious performance against others? Doing so can lead us to feel deserving of more than God has given us. Today, combat jealousy and discontentment by remembering God's favor toward you. We have only to look at Calvary's cross: "He was pierced for our transgressions; he was crushed for our iniquities; upon him was the chastisement that brought us peace, and with his wounds we are healed (Is 53:5)."

Prayer Continue to ask God to expose attitudes of jealousy toward others. Pray for anyone who comes to mind right now. Praise God for the work he is doing in and through them and ask him to help them use their resources for God's glory and the good of his kingdom. Then, ask God to expose feelings of discontentment toward him. Ask him for eyes to see all that he done for you in Jesus so that you might live joyfully.

Day 23

Rich Fool

Luke 12:13-21

Over the last three days of our study, we have examined our relationship with money as Kingdom residents. We have seen the tendency of our hearts to love and serve money, to become jealous when others prosper, and to become discontent when we imagine ourselves deserving of a greater measure of God's financial blessing. Ultimately, we have been confronted with Jesus' words, "You cannot serve God and money (Lk 16:13)." Today's parable reveals that our perspective of money shapes our use of money.

It was another typical day in the life of Jesus. He was teaching a large crowd that had gathered to hear his message about life in the kingdom of God. In fact, Luke tells us that "so many thousands of people had gathered together that they were trampling one another (Lk 12:1)." Suddenly, a man shouted at Jesus, "Teacher, tell my brother to divide the inheritance with me (v. 13)." After making his demand, I imagine the man shuffling his brother to the front of the group or pointing at him accusingly. To have interrupted Jesus, the speaker must have really thought he was in the right and expected Jesus to take his side in the brotherly dispute. Jesus' response was quick: "Man, who made me a judge or arbitrator over you (v. 14)?" While he was perfectly wise, Jesus decided not to engage in the debate over the man's family estate. Instead, he chose to re-

Kingdom Fruits

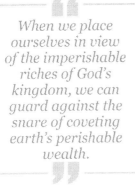

> When we place ourselves in view of the imperishable riches of God's kingdom, we can guard against the snare of coveting earth's perishable wealth.

veal the underlying issue and the eternal stakes of our perspective on money and possessions.

He began, "Take care, and be on your guard against all covetousness (v. 15)." The word "covetousness" means greedy desires. Here, Jesus addressed the underlying source of the brotherly conflict. The speaker's desire to gain some of his brother's rightful inheritance was a covetous desire. While we are not given the details of the dispute, it is easy to imagine why a man would want to tap into his brother's inheritance. Maybe, like the prodigal son, he had already blown his own inheritance. Maybe the law and custom of the time dictated that the older brother inherit the whole sum. Either way, the man desired something that was not his to possess.

Jesus' next words reveal something about the man's motivations for wanting a piece of his brother's inheritance and something fundamental about coveting. He said, be on guard against covetousness, "for one's life does not consist in the abundance of his possessions (v. 15)." Here, we see that the root of coveting is believing that abundant life can be found in abundant possessions. We in modern culture are acutely aware of this concept because society maintains that we are defined by our possessions, pleasures, and power and should, therefore, desire to acquire more and more.

Just watch old Super Bowl commercials and consider the consistency of their messages: "Your life is incomplete; you would be happier if you had the right car, candy, broker, website developer, or drink." The subliminal message is clear: "If you only had this product, then your life would have significance." In recent years, the overt messages may have changed – "Your life *is* complete. *You* are enough!" – but the subliminal message is the same: "If only you had the right car, candy, broker, website developer, or drink, you could really change the world, write your

Day 23

own story, or be whoever you want to be." In the new social economy, possessing the "right" stuff plus exhibiting the "right" behaviors gives our lives significance. A meaningful life can be bought and signaled to the rest of society.

But, looking for life in what this world offers is as old as time itself. Consider Eve, who desired the promise of god-likeness, even if she had to eat the fruit of tree of the knowledge of good and evil to get it. Or Jacob, who wanted the blessings of his brother Esau's birthright, even if he had to deceive his father to get it. David desired the pleasure of sleeping with his friend's wife, even if he had to kill him to get it, and Ananias wanted the prestige and affirmation of his church, even if he had to lie to get it. They believed a meaningful life could be purchased and were willing to pay costly prices to obtain the objects of their greedy desires.

Jesus' message is counter-cultural both then and now. He said, "Your life does *not* consist in the abundance of your possessions (v. 15, my paraphrase)." His message to the coveting brother is the same as his message to us. Neither possessions nor the power and prestige they afford can provide peace in this life or true riches in the next. To illustrate this point, Jesus told a parable about a rich farmer.

He said, "The land of a rich man produced plentifully, and he thought to himself, 'What shall I do, for I have nowhere to store my crops?' And he said, 'I will do this: I will tear down my barns and build larger ones, and there I will store all my grain and my goods. And I will say to my soul, "Soul, you have ample goods laid up for many years; relax, eat, drink, be merry."' But God said to him, 'Fool! This night your soul is required of you, and the things you have prepared, whose will they be (vv. 16-20)?'"

The root of coveting is believing that abundant life can be found in abundant possessions.

Notice, first, that the problem is not the rich man's wealth. Jesus does not condemn the man for having earthly wealth or the

Kingdom Fruits

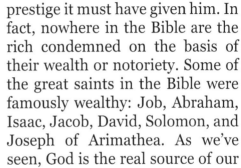

> *Neither possessions nor the power and prestige they afford can provide peace in this life or true riches in the next.*

prestige it must have given him. In fact, nowhere in the Bible are the rich condemned on the basis of their wealth or notoriety. Some of the great saints in the Bible were famously wealthy: Job, Abraham, Isaac, Jacob, David, Solomon, and Joseph of Arimathea. As we've seen, God is the real source of our financial resources. God had blessed the rich farmer with land, barns, and resources to plant and harvest crops. God provided good weather for the seed to grow and protection against insects and drought. The farmer's windfall harvest wouldn't have been possible apart from God's blessings. Since God himself distributes wealth according to his purposes and plans, he does not then condemn those he blesses for possessing those resources.

The problem, then, was with the farmer's use of his wealth. When faced with a decision about what to do with the excess crops from his plentiful harvest, he decided to build larger barns to store the extra grain and goods. On its face, the man's plan to expand his farming operation wasn't sinful. After all, the Bible does not prohibit building barns to facilitate one's resource management, and the Bible consistently encourages being a wise money-manager. But, Jesus revealed the rich farmer's selfish motives for storing his resources—to "relax, eat, drink, and be merry (v. 19)." Six times he uses the word "I" to describe himself and his plan. All he could think about was the life of leisure that awaited him once he had big enough barns to store more resources.

The farmer's sinful choice to hoard his wealth originated in false perspectives. First, he believed that he owned all that God had given him to steward and could, therefore, do with it whatever he pleased. Second, the rich fool fixated on earthly resources because he believed that his life consisted of the abundance of his possessions. He bought the lie that having more would give him freedom from the anxieties wrapped up in daily provision and sustenance:

Day 23

"I will say to my soul, 'Soul, you have ample goods laid up for many years; relax (v. 19).'" To him, storehouses of goods meant peace. It represented the good life. But, Jesus shared God's response to the man's perspectives and choices: "You fool!"

Jesus called his perspective foolish because life does not consist in our possessions. What the rich fool didn't know was that he was going to die before the new barns could be completed and the excess resources could be enjoyed. His money would be left to others, who like the brother in the crowd, would selfishly fight over it. Jesus concluded his story with this simple statement: "So is the one who lays up treasure for himself but is not rich toward God (v. 21)." In other words, seeking life in earthly possessions, which the thief of death steals fully and finally, is utterly foolish.

Where, then, do we find abundant life? After he concluded his parable, Jesus turned to his disciples. He said, "Therefore I tell you, do not be anxious about your life, what you will eat, nor about your body, what you will put on. For life is *more* than food, and the body more than clothing...Do not seek what you are to eat and what you are to drink, nor be worried. For all the nations of the world seek after these things, and your Father knows that you need them. Instead, seek his kingdom and these things will be added to you (vv. 22-23, emphasis mine; vv. 29-31)." Jesus again shifts our perspective. The world says the good life is found in what we possess and that the more we have stored up, the more peace we will experience. Jesus says that abundant life is found in seeking his kingdom.

How we steward our resources, then, is an external manifestation of our internal beliefs about where abundant life can be found. Only when we believe that life is found in seeking his kingdom can we be rich toward God,

Take care, and be on your guard against all covetousness, for one's life does not consist in the abundance of his possessions.

Kingdom Fruits

using our resources to advance his kingdom. Jesus concluded his message with a hopeful vision of seeking first the kingdom: "Fear not, little flock, for it is your Father's good pleasure to give you the kingdom. Sell your possessions, and give to the needy. Provide yourselves with moneybags that do not grow old, with a treasure in the heavens that does not fail, where no thief approaches and no moth destroys (vv. 32-33)." When we place ourselves in view of the imperishable riches of God's kingdom, we can guard against the snare of coveting earth's perishable wealth (1 Tim 6:9-10). When we trust God's daily provision and sustenance, we don't need to hoard what we have. When we set our hope on God for peace in this life and the next, we can "do good," be "rich in good works," be "generous," and be "ready to share" (1 Tim 6:17-18). In so doing, we store up treasures for ourselves "as a good foundation for the future" so that we may "take hold of that which is *truly life* (1 Tim 6:19, emphasis mine).

Day 23

Food for Thought

Martyred missionary Jim Elliot spent his life sharing the gospel with the unreached. He famously said, "He is no fool who gives up what he cannot keep to gain what he cannot lose." Consider how his words contrast the rich fool's: "I will store all my grains and goods." Examine your own perspective on your resources, possessions, and very life. Do you treat them as if they were "unkeepable"? Are you spending them to build God's kingdom or are you trying to store them? God's Word reveals one plan to be utterly foolish and the other to be wholly wise.

Faith in Action

Wisdom sees all that we have as temporary blessings from God which belong to him. Through that lens, we can follow God's revealed plan for our financial stewardship: tithing 10% and planning to be generous with the remaining 90%. Freewill offerings to Kingdom endeavors and radical generosity to others in need reveal a loose grip on earthly treasure and a tight hold on life that is really life (1 Tim 6:19). If you struggle in these areas, talk to a pastor about accessing practical resources for planning to be obedient and generous.

Prayer

As you pray today, ask God to reveal any covetous desires to build or hoard resources for security or significance. Thank him for promising to provide for and sustain your life for as many days as he wills you to live on the earth. Praise him for promising true, lasting treasure in heaven, and commit anew to seek first his kingdom on earth.

Day 24

Good Samaritan Part One

Luke 10:25-37

Our natural inclination is to avoid unpleasantness. Toddlers provide compelling evidence of this innate tendency. When confronted with broccoli, a dirty diaper, or a literal fall-on-face situation, the negative reaction is swift and strong. Given the choice, we choose meals that taste good, couches that feel good, clothes that look good, and candles that cover a multitude of smells. When confronted with unpleasantness, our tendency is to take action to put distance between ourselves and the encounter. The best word to describe this movement is "repulsion," which paints the image of one being driven back by a powerful force.

    Think about what repulses you. Maybe you remember the street dumpster that taught you, having once walked near it, to use the other side of the street to avoid the foul odors. Perhaps your mind goes to the company party or class reunion where you take pains to avoid that one person who traps you in conversation about himself or looks for opportunities to belittle others. Maybe you think of scary critters, open wounds, death or the dying, disease or the diseased. When confronted with the repulsive, our natural inclination is to take a step back. In today's par-

Kingdom Fruits

God sent his only son into enemy territory.

able, Jesus reveals that radical compassion takes a step forward.

Jesus was teaching one day when a lawyer interrupted him with an important question: "Teacher, what shall I do to inherit eternal life (v. 25)?" This is a great question to ask, but the text reveals that he wasn't seeking an answer for his soul; he simply wanted to test Jesus. Rather than answer the question, Jesus asked one of his own: "What is written in the Law? How do you read it (v. 26)?" I imagine this sudden cross-examination from Jesus may have caught the lawyer off guard. Nonetheless, after a moment's reflection, the lawyer responded with these words: "You shall love the Lord your God with all your heart and with all your soul and with all your strength and with all your mind, and your neighbor as yourself (v. 27)."

Jesus looked at the attorney and spoke, "You have answered correctly; do this, and you will live (v. 28)." He let the words hang in the air as he continued to study the lawyer. He began to get uncomfortable as he looked at Jesus. Somehow, he knew that Jesus could see straight through him, and his pretenses began to fall away. He knew in his heart that loving both God and his neighbor like that was impossible. If it were up to him to justify himself through perfect keeping of the Law, he would fall short every time. But, remember, he wasn't looking for truth; he was trying to trip up this new teacher on the scene. He could feel the people around them staring at him. He wasn't about to lose face to this uneducated carpenter. So, seeking to justify himself and his life, he asked one more question: "And who is my neighbor (v. 29)?"

Jesus paused, keenly aware of the large group of people that had gathered to witness their conversation. The people were looking at Jesus now, too. They knew the expected answer to this question, just like the attorney. The Jewish religious leaders had taught them that their

Day 24

neighbors were fellow religious Jews. They were the ones who were to be loved as oneself. Tax collectors, prostitutes, criminals, Samaritans, and Gentiles were sinners—not neighbors—so, the law's requirement to love neighbors as oneself didn't apply. The group waited for Jesus to answer the question. Jesus told a story instead.

"A man was traveling down from Jerusalem to Jericho, when he was attacked suddenly by a band of thieves. They robbed him, beat him nearly to death, and left him to die on the road. As chance would have it, a Jewish priest appeared, but seeing the man lying in the road, he walked around him and continued on. Soon, a Levite appeared, but he too avoided the man in favor of his journey. Finally, a Samaritan appeared. Rather than pass by, he approached the man, applied wine and oil to his wounds, placed him on his donkey, and led him to an inn. Once there, he gave the innkeeper money to care for the injured man until he returned from his trip. He even promised to cover any additional costs upon his return (vv. 30-35, my paraphrase)."

Jesus finished the story and looked at the crowd. I imagine it was so quiet you could hear the sound of people breathing. The expressions on their faces registered shock or anger. They understood what Jesus was saying, and it was the opposite of everything they had been taught. The priest and the Levite were representatives of the ruling religious class in Israel. They were the ones who should have been modeling what it meant to love one's neighbor as oneself.

Yet, in this story, when confronted with the opportunity to show compassion to a foreigner, they ignored him. It's easy to imagine how they justified their decision to pass by. Maybe they were on their way to accomplish an urgent ministry responsibility. Maybe they were fearful that the same fate would befall them if they paused to help. Perhaps they misjudged the cause, imagining the

Jesus willingly entered a broken and stained world and drew near to the unclean.

Kingdom Fruits

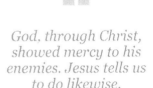

God, through Christ, showed mercy to his enemies. Jesus tells us to do likewise.

man on the roadside to be a no-good scoundrel who got what he deserved. Or, maybe they had seen this happen to so many people on the road to Jericho that they just didn't care anymore.

These rationales may feel familiar to us; perhaps we have even used the same logic in similar situations. But, a dying man? Most of us feel confident that we would step in and help if someone's life was on the line. So, what gives?

By Old Testament law, one who touched someone who was bloody, sick, or dead became ceremonially unclean. One who was unclean could not serve in the temple or offer sacrifices until they performed ritual washings and waited the dictated time period for their restoration to cleanness—up to as many as seven days. Avoiding uncleanness was the most convenient way to keep a personal calendar unaltered. Seen another way, avoiding uncleanness was a pathway to the kind of heightened external holiness that could be measured against others to puff oneself up. In Matthew 23, Jesus proclaims a series of "woes" against the religious elite's hypocrisy, including their false understanding of uncleanness: "Woe to you, scribes and Pharisees, hypocrites! For you are like whitewashed tombs, which outwardly appear beautiful, but within are full of dead people's bones and all uncleanness. So you also outwardly appear righteous to others, but within you are full of hypocrisy and lawlessness (vv. 27-28)." Whether out of convenience or a desire to maintain a carefully coifed image of righteousness, the two men in the parable whose knowledge of God should have prompted them to extend mercy to the beaten man, sadly, did not.

That left the Samaritan. Jesus' audience would have cringed when they thought about the word; most of them wouldn't actually say it out loud. The Jews and Samaritans had been hostile neighbors for centuries. When the Jews were taken to Babylon as captives in 586 BC, some were

Day 24

allowed to remain in the Israel. Many Jewish men who remained chose to marry Gentile women. The descendants of these people became the Samaritans. They formed their own community and created their own system of worship. Over time, the Samaritans and the Jews became enemies and treated one another with animosity and hatred. They avoided one another like the plague, often refusing to travel through the other's territory. That is what made Jesus' parable so troubling.

After all, a Samaritan was the last guy on earth that one would expect to help a Jew. Yet, in this story, he is the one who had compassion on the helpless traveler. Obviously a successful businessman, he broke out his travel bag and began to treat the man's wounds—wine to cleanse the wounds from infection and oil to provide a soothing salve. He hoisted the man's dead weight up onto his donkey, while he chose to walk the laborious journey to the inn. After getting him settled into a room, the Samaritan paid the innkeeper the equivalent of two days' salary for a day-laborer. This was more than enough to cover his expenses for several weeks. Then, he promised to return and cover any additional expenses the man might accumulate. This was an amazing act of love. The Samaritan drew near to his enemy. He embraced the inconvenience of his schedule change, risked his life to help the injured man, and incurred the cost of his care. Few people would do this for a countryman, let alone an enemy.

Jesus' audience may have been shocked by his story of the Samaritan's radical compassion toward an unlikely recipient. They may have felt convicted by the many times they had not shown mercy to their own friends let alone their enemies. However, they likely did not yet understand that in redefining neighborhood, Jesus was also drawing a parallel to his own saving work. Consider who we were. Because of our sin, we were enemies of God (Rom 5:10). Justice

Jesus possesses the power and authority to pour out God's mercy to the uttermost.

would have permitted God to walk on the other side of the road, leaving us to die without knowing him. Pronounced dead in our sins on the roadside (Eph 2:1), we did not possess the strength to save or heal ourselves (Rom 5:6). But God, in his mercy, did not pass us by. He did not look dispassionately on our helpless and hopeless souls. God sent his only son into enemy territory.

Like the Samaritan, Jesus embraced inconvenience to show radical compassion to his enemies. Jesus left behind the holiness of heaven where no sin, pain, or suffering threatens the peace and pleasure of God's glorious presence. He took on flesh and dwelt among sinners. While on earth, Jesus himself never sinned; yet, the effects of sin pressed in on him – sickness, sorrow, betrayal, loss (Heb 4:15). Given the choice, would we not bypass the stains of sin's pervasive influence? Yet, Jesus willingly entered a broken and stained world and drew near to the unclean.

Like the Samaritan, Jesus risked his life to save his enemies. Throughout his ministry, Jesus spoke of his coming sacrificial death (Lk 13:33; Mt 16:21; Mt 17:22; Mk 8:31). Jesus understood the cost of his mission on earth. He knew that to restore sinners to right standing before God, a sinless substitute must be offered on their behalf. Jesus understood that Isaiah 53 spoke of him: "But he was pierced for our transgressions; he was crushed for our iniquities; upon him was the chastisement that brought us peace, and with his wounds we are healed. All we like sheep have gone astray; we have turned—every one—to his own way; and the Lord has laid on him the iniquity of us all (Is 53:6)." Jesus knew the cost of radical compassion and willingly offered his own life as a ransom for many.

In today's parable, the parallel between the Good Samaritan's compassion and Christ's are many. But, let us glory a moment in the key differences. Despite his costly compassion, the Samaritan lacked the power to guarantee ultimate healing for the beaten man by the roadside. He graciously paid for his stay at the hotel, but he could not personally oversee the man's healing because he had to be about his business. He promised to return to check in on

Day 24

the man's recovery, but he lacked the authority to guarantee his own safe return to the inn.

On the other hand, Jesus possesses the power and authority to pour out God's mercy to the uttermost. Jesus doesn't merely bind our physical bodies; he restores our souls to eternal fellowship with God. Jesus doesn't just situate us in a hotel and go about his business; he gives us an eternal home as sons and daughters in the family of God. While we wait for full and final healing, we do so in his very presence—not just by our bedside, but in our hearts (Col 1:27). Secure in his presence, we can trust his promises – to return, to intercede for us, to present us blameless – because he is Almighty God. This is cause for great rejoicing! God, through Christ, showed mercy to his enemies. Jesus tells us to do likewise.

At the conclusion of his parable, Jesus asked the attorney a final question: "Which of these three, do you think, proved to be a neighbor to the man who fell among the robbers (v. 36)?" Now it was the lawyer's turn to pause. Unwittingly, he had been hooked by Jesus' story. What began as self-justification had ended in self-condemnation. Still proud, he refused even to say the word "Samaritan." He said instead, "The one who showed him mercy." As he turned to leave, Jesus replied, "You go, and do likewise (v. 37)."

Tomorrow, we will study ways in which we can live out the fruit of Christ's mercy in our daily lives. As we conclude today's study, consider this glorious truth: Jesus fulfilled the law perfectly, loving God and neighbor at all times with all of his heart. As a result, when the Lord laid all of our sins on his shoulders at the cross, his sacrifice was accepted by God on our behalf. When we believe in his finished work on the cross and in his victorious resurrection, God applies the righteousness of Christ to our accounts. In God's eyes, it is as if we, too, fulfilled the law, perfectly loving God and our neighbors. This is mysterious and amazing grace!

Kingdom Fruits

Food for Thought When you read the parable of the Good Samaritan, which character do you usually identify with? We tend to feel convicted by our own propensity to bypass those in need. That is an important discussion which we will have tomorrow. Today, take time to reflect on the helpless man on the roadside. Read Romans 5:6-11, and note the parallels between our condition before Christ and the injured man's condition. Consider anew God's mercy toward you, and rejoice in his work of reconciliation in your life.

Faith in Action Our desire for comfort often pushes us to avoid difficult conversations, people, and situations. Throughout the day, take care to notice your reactions and impulses to unpleasantness. In those moments, call to mind a visual image of Jesus moving toward you in all of your brokenness, and look for opportunities to move toward those in your path who are hurting and in need of his love–and yours.

Prayer As you talk with the Father today, thank him for sending Jesus into our uncleanness. Thank him for moving toward us, rescuing us, and being with us while we wait for full and final restoration in his presence. Ask him to flood your heart with gratitude for his mercy and to prepare your heart to extend radical compassion to the people in your life.

Good Samaritan Part Two

Luke 10:25-37

Yesterday, we studied the mercy of God poured out on us, the hopeless and helpless, the broken and bruised. Through the parable of the Good Samaritan, Jesus revealed the depths of his compassion for us and his willingness to take our uncleanness upon himself that we might receive his cleanness before God. What a gift! Jesus also redefined the concept of "neighbor" for a prejudiced audience. Our neighbors are not only those who look like us, act like us, and live like us; our neighbors are those who look different, act different, and live different. Whom we perceive to be enemies, Jesus calls neighbors. Just as he showed unmerited mercy to his enemies, Jesus tells us to go and do likewise.

In a broken world full of pain and suffering, where do we begin? What does it look like to extend radical mercy to our neighbors? First, we must pause to remember our motivation for doing so: those who have been shown great mercy show great mercy to others. As we have studied, the depth of our understanding of what we've been given in Christ shapes the depth of our desire to give to others. His inconvenient, risky, and costly compassion

Kingdom Fruits

> *In following Jesus' call to show radical mercy to our neighbors, we point them to who he is and what he has done for us.*

toward us leads us to show inconvenient, risky, and costly compassion toward our neighbors. Second, we must remember that our good works flow out of Christ who dwells in us. Even when gripped by a rightful motivation to show mercy, we may be tempted yet to misplace our confidence for showing mercy. If we place our confidence in ourselves, we will either languish under the guilt of our inevitable inadequacies or puff up with pride. Self-confidence severs us from God's power and deprives us of joy. Instead, our confidence for showing mercy is found in Jesus, the Merciful. As we abide in him, our lives will give evidence of the fruit of his righteousness.

Third, we must live with an awareness of those around us. In the parable, the Good Samaritan was headed somewhere—either to or from Jerusalem on the road to Jericho (v.30). I doubt he was expecting a schedule disruption that rendered him ceremonially unclean, wrecking his day's schedule and quite possibly his religious and social calendar. Rather than rationalize the urgency of his plans, he noticed the wounded man's distress and stepped in to help. Awareness enables us to notice the needs of others in order to show them mercy.

Finally, we must adopt a new vision of risk. When confronted with an opportunity to show mercy, our risk assessment usually includes financial calculations, personal safety checks, and reputation management. Our underlying question is, what are the risks if I engage this opportunity? But, what if our question was, what are the risks if I don't? Think again about the unrighteous wealth discussed in the parable of the dishonest manager. Earth's riches can be stolen, destroyed, depreciated, or lost. They cannot prevent disease, death, or disaster. What's more, they will not produce anything of value in eternity. God has made clear the risks associated with storing up treasures on earth. He does so not to guilt us into giving—re-

Day 25

member our motivation in Christ—but, in love, to urge us to do what he knows is best for us. Showing mercy to those in need is best for our hearts' affections toward God while we wait for the glorious coming of his eternal kingdom and best for our experiencing the true riches of Christ in that age. Risking some discomfort here on earth is infinitely worth the treasures gained in Christ's kingdom. As Jesus has taught us throughout the parables, following him sacrificially is costly... and priceless.

A right understanding of Jesus' costly and priceless mercy poured out on us, coupled with his call to "go and do likewise," leads us to the desire to show radical mercy to our neighbors. If it doesn't, a critical link in our understanding of Jesus and his mission is missing. When we become convinced of his heart for how we should love our neighbors, we can begin to feel overwhelmed by the numerous opportunities to give and serve. Thankfully, in Christ, we have the Holy Spirit within us to counsel us and stir us toward the roles he has for us. He also gives us his Word to help us exercise wisdom in our finances and godly scholars and pastors to guide our beliefs about the roles and contributions of the local church, parachurch organizations, communities, individuals, and government entities in alleviating suffering.[1] I'd like to provide a short example of one such grounding principle that helps me discern when to provide direct financial assistance to those who ask me. My prayer is that your heart will be simultaneously freed from guilt and moved to radical compassion for the hurting.

The grounding principle is this: Personal influence informs personal investment. Picture one or two scenarios in which you've been asked for money. You may picture a person on the street re-

> *Our underlying question is, what are the risks if I engage this opportunity? But, what if our question was, what are the risks if I don't?*

---

1. Corbett and Fikkert (2012) provide an excellent deep-dive on this topic in *When Helping Hurts,* Moody Publishers.

Kingdom Fruits

Those who have been shown great mercy show great mercy to others.

questing change, a person at the gas station requesting a fill-up, or a family member asking for a substantial loan. In the first two scenarios, you may not have the opportunity to develop any personal influence in their lives. Perhaps you encountered them on vacation or off the interstate. In those instances, we should follow the Holy Spirit's leading and look to give cold cups of water in Jesus' name (Mt 10:42).

Generally, though, when we receive requests to help people in need of financial assistance, it's from the people closest to us: our parents, brothers, sisters, kids, cousins, friends, co-workers, or fellow church members. With these individuals, we have personal influence and a pathway to discovering and speaking into the circumstances that led to the request. However, family pressure, guilt, or fear of conflict will often push us just to write a check to avoid the difficult conversation required to discern the circumstances of the stated need. Without that crucial step, we may be unwittingly enabling their poor stewardship and endangering our own. The money I foolishly give to the wrong person today may prevent me from having the money to wisely give to the right person tomorrow. Understanding the circumstances of the stated need, then, is critical to how we help. Sometimes those circumstances will be outside of their control—like a wave of difficulty through illness, job loss, housing loss (see Job). Other times, the situation may be born out of poor financial choices.

Once we are aware of any habitual mismanagement, our discernment criteria for giving direct financial assistance should include a demonstrated willingness to learn and implement new habits. Some may hesitate at the idea of "conditional" giving, but consider what is more loving: a doctor bandaging an infected wound and sending the patient away, or a doctor providing medication to treat the underlying infection that is causing the patient to suffer (before or alongside bandaging the wound)? When

Day 25

people who have made poor financial choices come to us and ask for money, they are really saying, "I know that I made the poor decision that got me into this fix, but I'd like you to spend your money to free me from the resulting consequences." Sending them on their way with a solution to the symptom but no medication for the root problem may cause less conflict, but it may actually hinder their financial health.

For those who are receptive to our influence, we have an opportunity to treat both the infection and the symptoms. As they work with me or other financial trainers, I am able to walk alongside them, encouraging them to abandon destructive habits and follow God's wisdom for our finances. Their willingness to do so shapes my financial investment. These steps require much more time and effort than writing a check, but the opportunity to show inconvenient, risky, and costly mercy is worthwhile. Kingdom investment yields eternal dividends. In following Jesus' call to show radical mercy to our neighbors, we point them to who he is and what he has done for us. We demonstrate a right understanding of earth's fleeting riches, treasuring instead the riches of Christ. And, we may get to share in our loved one's joy as they experience the freedom that accompanies wise resource management.

Financial assistance is just one of the ways we can show mercy to our neighbors. People are in need of encouragement, counsel, kindness, help, and love. Let us daily abide in Jesus, praying that our hearts may be filled with his compassion to notice and move toward the hurting and the helpless.

Kingdom investment yields eternal dividends.

Kingdom Fruits

Food for Thought Read Isaiah 58, and pay careful attention to the prophet's indictments against Israel. What do they reveal about God's heart for the hurting and downcast? As his chosen people, Israel was to serve as a signpost toward a just and righteous King who would come, not to be served but to serve (Mt 20:28). This glorious King has now been revealed to us in Christ. How much more should we, his covenant people, seek to reflect his compassion by showing mercy to our neighbors?

Faith in Action Reflect for a moment on the habits of your life. Can you remember the last time you endured personal inconvenience, risk, or cost to show mercy to a friend? An enemy? If not, think about what hinders you from following Jesus' call to "go and do likewise." What earthly concerns—like schedule, safety, security, or reputation— might you be elevating above Kingdom concerns? Today, look for opportunities to extend mercy in Jesus' name.

Prayer As you talk with God today, begin by rehearsing the story of Jesus' costly compassion toward you. Confess the tendency to elevate earthly concerns and put compassion on hold. Confess guilt or pride in your service to others, and re-center your motivation and confidence on Jesus. Ask for a mind to remember the mercy you have been shown that you might show it to others. Finally, ask for eyes to see your neighbors' needs, feet to move toward them, and hands to help.

Day 26

Unforgiving Servant

Matthew 18:21-35

Have you ever had someone hurt you in a deep and lasting way? If you're like me, the answer to that question is a resounding "Yes!" Because we live in a broken world filled with sinful people, we routinely find ourselves in situations where we are hurt by the words or actions of others. Sometimes these hurts are relatively mild; other times, they scar us for life. Honestly, I could provide numerous illustrations from my own life experiences, and I bet you could too.

When we encounter these situations, our natural reaction is retribution. We want to inflict the same type of hurt on those who have hurt us. We may want to lash out in anger or plot some type of revenge. Left unresolved, this hurt will slowly turn into a cancer-like resentment that will fill us with bitterness. Ultimately, our lives may be more affected by this lingering anger than by the initial hurtful experience.

Jesus' disciples struggled with forgiveness, too. One day, Peter asked Jesus a penetrating question: "How often will my brother sin against me, and I forgive him? As many as seven times (v. 21)?" Peter was trying to figure out the same thing we are—what is forgiveness, and how often do I have to extend it to someone? To his credit, he was being generous. The religious teaching of his day said that he

Kingdom Fruits

There should be no limits to our forgiveness.

must only forgive another person three times for the same offense. He was offering seven! Jesus' response must have caught him off-guard. Jesus said, "I do not say to you seven times, but seventy-seven times (v. 22)." Can you imagine the look on Peter's face? He must have thought, "I have to, what?"

Here, Jesus introduced an important principle at work in his kingdom: there should be no limits to our forgiveness. To reinforce his point, he told a fascinating story. He said that a king wanted to settle accounts with his servants, so he brought in a man who owed him a debt of 10,000 talents. In Jesus' day, a talent represented a significant amount of money. One talent of silver was equal to 6,000 denarii, which was the equivalent of 20 years of salary for a common laborer. When you multiply that by ten, you realize that Jesus was talking about an incomprehensible debt that the man couldn't hope to pay. As a result, the king was preparing to sell the man, his family, and all that they had to recoup some of his loss. Facing this devastating future, the man fell to his knees and begged the king for mercy. Moved with compassion, the king forgave his debt and released him from his obligation.

Forgiven and free, the man turned his attention to his own affairs. In need of money, he went to see another man that owed him a small debt of 100 denarii, which was the equivalent of about three months' wages for a common laborer. When the man heard that he didn't have his money, he went into a rage, choking the man and demanding that he pay what he owed. This man also fell to his knees and pleaded for mercy, but his pleas fell on deaf ears. The man who had been forgiven so much threw him into debtors' prison until his debt could be paid in full.

The king was enraged when he heard what the man had done. Immediately, he had him brought to the castle and rebuked him. "You wicked servant! I forgave you all that debt because you pleaded with me. And should not

Day 26

Forgiveness is covering the sins of others in the same way that God covers our own sin.

you have had mercy on your fellow servant, as I had mercy on you (vv. 32-33)?" Then, he sent the man to debtors' prison for the rest of his life. Jesus ended the parable with these words, "So also my heavenly Father will do to every one of you, if you do not forgive your brother from your heart (v. 35)."

This story is easy to understand but hard to apply to our own lives. Clearly, the king in the story is God the Father. When we place our faith in Jesus' finished work on our behalf, God the Father provides us with complete forgiveness (Eph 1:3-14; Col 2:14). As we walk in relationship with him, God continues to forgive us every time we rebel against his truth, choosing to sin (1 Jn 1:9). God's forgiveness is limitless, and he expects our capacity to offer forgiveness to match his own. Jesus spoke about this in Matthew 6:14-15 as well: "For if you forgive others their trespasses, your heavenly Father will also forgive you, but if you do not forgive others their trespasses, neither will your Father forgive your trespasses." Jesus taught us here that God's daily forgiveness of our sins against him is dependent upon our daily forgiveness of those who sin against us. As a result, our understanding and practice of forgiveness is critical to our spiritual growth as disciples.

So, what is forgiveness? Here is my definition: "Forgiveness is covering the sins of others in the same way that God covers our own sin." I like this definition because it reminds me of the way that God has dealt with my sin. He chooses to forgive it and forever remove it from his thoughts about me. It also reminds me that I must make the same choice when someone hurts me. This process of forgiveness requires several specific steps.

We must choose to forgive, so that our own relationship with God will be unhindered.

First, we must forsake our right to revenge. Remember, when

Kingdom Fruits

Forgiveness is a difficult command to obey, but it is a clear command for every Kingdom resident.

we are hurt, we are tempted to hurt back. When I truly forgive someone, I give up my "right" to retribution, no matter how justified I may feel in my response. After all, if it's necessary, vengeance is God's work. Paul wrote, "Beloved, never avenge yourselves, but leave it to the wrath of God, for it is written, 'Vengeance is mine, I will repay,' says the Lord … Do not be overcome by evil, but overcome evil with good (Rom 12:19, 21)." God wants us to practice forgiveness and leave any retribution to him. Second, we must choose to grant the same kind of forgiveness that we've been given by God. As today's parable reveals, God has forgiven us an immeasurable debt— one that we could never pay—through the free gift of his grace and mercy. He has removed it from us, figuratively speaking, as far as the east is from the west (Ps 103:12). When we are wronged, he wants us to pour out forgiveness through grace and mercy, too. True forgiveness allows us to encounter those individuals in the future without digging up the pain of the past.

Third, we must pursue reconciliation to the degree possible. There are two ways we can forgive someone. First, we can simply choose to cover their sin (1 Pet 4:8). This is the best approach when dealing with the kind of superficial wrongs that we often encounter on a daily basis. In love, we can choose to forgive and move on. Second, we can choose to confront someone because of his or her sin. This is the proper approach for more hurtful sins— the kind that we can't seem to cover. In these instances, we should go to them to explain how their actions have hurt us. Of course, we would desire some expression of repentance and contrition so that we might grant forgiveness in a redemptive and reconciling way

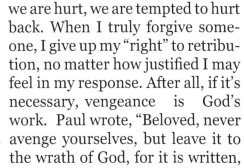

Loving my neighbor means many things, including giving people a break and keeping forgiveness on "autopilot" in my life.

Day 26

(Mt 18:15-20). Yet, we are commanded to forgive, regardless of someone's response.

It is important to understand that forgiveness does not immediately restore trust. Depending on the grievousness of the sin, trust may never be able to be restored in the relationship. Similarly, forgiveness does not mean the absence of consequences. Some sins are so terrible, some hurts so deep, that the relationship cannot continue the way that it did before the sin occurred. Still, we must choose to forgive, so that our own relationship with God will be unhindered. We must leave the vengeance to God.

Fourth, we must pray for the person that we have forgiven. This is another indication that authentic forgiveness has occurred. We should pray that God will reach into his or her heart and do a life-transforming work. We should pray for salvation or sanctification to occur for the glory of God. And, we should pray that we would bury the sin completely, so that its pain will not recapture our hearts.

Forgiveness is a difficult command to obey, but it is a clear command for every Kingdom resident. Ultimately, our ability to forgive is dependent upon understanding two important truths. First, God has forgiven us so much—how could we be unwilling to forgive others? Unlike the man in today's parable, I must both receive and extend grace. Second, we have sinned against so many other people. Why should we be surprised when people sin against us? Loving my neighbor includes giving people a break and keeping forgiveness on "autopilot" in my life. When I live in the reality of these truths, I will find that granting forgiveness becomes much easier to do!

Kingdom Fruits

Food for Thought — Today's parable is challenging because it examines an area of our discipleship that is difficult to face—our own unwillingness to forgive others. We've all been hurt by others. Are you struggling to forgive someone today? Who is it? What did he or she do? When we refuse to cover others' sin like God covers ours, we are usurping his role as Righteous Judge and standing in opposition to his commands. Read Matthew 7. Reflect on the posture of humility required to extend forgiveness to those who wrong us.

Faith in Action — It's time to do something about any lack of forgiveness that may be lingering in your heart. Grant forgiveness through grace and mercy by either covering the sin or by confronting it. It is time to be free from the anger, resentment, or bitterness that is living in your heart because of this situation. If you need help, call a pastor or counselor and begin the process of forgiveness.

Prayer — As you pray today, talk with God about the struggles you may be having in granting forgiveness to someone. First, confess any bitterness or grudges you may be holding. Then, share your burdens with your Father. He cares for you (1 Pet 5:6-7) and empathizes with your hurts (Heb 4:15). Thank him for promising to right wrongs and restore perfect justice in his eternal presence (Rev 21:1-8). Finally, ask for patience to endure the brokenness until he comes, forgiving others as God, in Christ, has forgiven you (Eph 4:32).

Day 27

Persistent Friend Part One

Luke 11:1-13

  I'll never forget the last time I was stranded on the side of the road. My wife Lyla and I, along with our daughters Cherie and Cassie, were traveling from Mobile, AL to Orlando, FL. Our girls had been competing with their university tennis team at a national championship. When the tournament was over, we loaded everything into our van and headed for Disney World. On the long drive through the Florida panhandle, I recognized the telltale signs of a flat tire. It felt like a thousand degrees on the side of the interstate as we waited on a wrecker. Three hours and two new tires later, we finally resumed our journey. Now, I'm the proud member of AAA, and I have the peace of mind that comes from knowing that I'll have help should I find myself in a situation like that again.
  I have many such protections in my life, and I would imagine that you do, too. I have a fire extinguisher in my kitchen, fire alarms throughout my house, and a hose near the diesel tank on my farm. We can purchase insurance for just about anything—our lives, health, property, teeth, jewelry, travel—even small appliances from Wal-Mart. The list seems endless. Each is designed to protect us in the event of an emergency, but we rarely use them. If we're

Kingdom Fruits

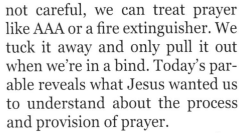

> The prayer for daily bread is an expression of our need for and confidence in God's provision in every area of our lives.

not careful, we can treat prayer like AAA or a fire extinguisher. We tuck it away and only pull it out when we're in a bind. Today's parable reveals what Jesus wanted us to understand about the process and provision of prayer.

One day, Jesus returned to his disciples after spending time alone in prayer. When he arrived, one of his disciples asked him, "Lord, teach us to pray, as John taught his disciples (v. 1)." I'm sure that Jesus was thrilled with this question! His reply was quick and concise. He said, "When you pray, say: Father, hallowed be your name. Your kingdom come. Give us each day our daily bread, and forgive us our sins, for we ourselves forgive everyone who is indebted to us. And lead us not into temptation (vv. 2-4)."

Perhaps you notice something familiar about these verses. It is a condensed version of the Lord's Prayer as recorded by Matthew (6:9-13). This is often called the "model prayer" because it provides us with a template for prayer. In it, Jesus identified five categories that help to shape our prayers. First, he identified worship. We are celebrating God's character when we acknowledge and exalt his name. A true understanding of God's worth will always point our heart's endless flow of worship toward him. Second, he identified surrender. Jesus reminded us that God is the sovereign King of all creation, and as a result, we should yield our lives to his Kingdom purposes for us. Third, he identified dependence. The prayer for daily bread is an expression of our need for and confidence in God's provision in every area of our lives. Fourth, Jesus identified forgiveness. We are redeemed sinners, and sinner's sin. As a result, we must pause daily to clear the air. Confession allows us to do that. And, it reminds us that we need to forgive the people who've sinned against us. Fifth, and finally, he identified grace. Our battle with sin begins with a battle against temptation. Prayer reminds us that

Day 27

we are susceptible to temptation; grace reminds us that God is big enough to deliver us from it.

Unlike Matthew's account, Luke records the illustration Jesus used to coach his disciples on prayer. Naturally, Jesus used a parable to help them understand it. The story's main character has a significant problem. A visiting friend has arrived at his home in the middle of the night. Perhaps the friend was expected at a later time or maybe his visit was unexpected. Either way, in a world without phones or Internet, there was no way to predict when he would arrive, and the host was woefully unprepared. Now to us, this may seem like a minor inconvenience, but in that day it was a huge problem. A host in Jesus' day was expected to welcome guests with food and wine, regardless of the hour. In fact, it was a shame upon one's name and family to do otherwise. You can imagine how panicked he must have felt when his friend knocked on the front door.

After welcoming his guest and getting him situated, he excused himself and slipped out the back door. Then, he raced down the street to another friend's house. Even though it was midnight, he knocked on the door. "Hey, I need some help," and he proceeded to tell his friend the story through the closed door. His friend replied, "Leave me alone. We're already in bed and the kids are asleep. Go away." Any other time he might have given up, but this was an emergency. The host continued to knock on the door relentlessly. "Please, help me." Finally, knowing that this could go on all night and would eventually wake up his family, the man's friend rose and gave him the food that he needed for his guest. We can only imagine the host's gratitude for this gift of grace. "I owe you one, bro," he probably called out as he rushed back towards home.

> *Prayer reminds us that we are susceptible to temptation; grace reminds us that God is big enough to deliver us from it.*

Then Jesus taught the lesson of the parable: "And I tell you, ask, and it will be given to you; seek, and you will find; knock, and it will be opened to you. For every-

Kingdom Fruits

> In our need, we are to come to God; in response, he promises to hear and to meet us with an open door.

one who asks receives, and the one who seeks finds, and to the one who knocks it will be opened (vv. 9-10)." Here, Jesus puts us in the shoes of the host who persistently knocks on his friend's door until he receives help. He uses the active images of asking, seeking, and knocking to explain the process and provision of prayer. In our need, we are to come to God; in response, he promises to hear and to meet us with an open door. What a life-giving truth.

Consider the described process and resulting provision in the parable. First, the host approached his friend's house in humility, aware of his urgent need. Had he believed that he had it all under control, refusing to seek help, he may have felt an initial boost of pride—"See? I got this; I don't need anyone." However, when his guest sat at his table, he would have had nothing to set before him. Believing himself to be capable was not sufficient to produce food and wine for his guest. Asking for help required him to admit his need for help and to abandon the image that he could provide for himself. In the same way, coming to God in prayer requires an understanding of our need for him. When we do not pray, we fail to see the limits of our resources, believing that our wisdom, power, and ability to control people and situations are sufficient to sustain us. We "lean on our own understanding (Prov 3:5)," which cuts us off from God's power at work through us. Jesus identified the remedy: ask, seek, and knock.

Second, the host approached his friend's house with confidence in his friend's character and resources. Knocking on his door persistently indicated his belief that his friend's care for him would lead him to hear his need

> Prayer is supposed to be an every moment, every day practice.

Day 27

and desire to help. It also demonstrated his knowledge that his friend was the kind of person who always had extra loaves baked and extra bottles in the cellar. The desperate host went to the friend with the heart *and* the resources to help him in his hour of need. We should approach God with the same confidence that he stands ready to hear our cries and help us. Sometimes, it is not pride but shame that keeps us from coming to God in prayer. Maybe we feel unworthy to speak to a holy God, or we feel that we need to clean up our act a little bit before we ask for his help. We fear his disapproval and, so, avoid his presence. But, shame and fear are dismantled by Jesus' words to the wary: ask, seek, knock.

As we grow in our knowledge of and relationship with God, we learn that he is a God who loves to commune with us—so much so that he sent Jesus to die in our place to make it possible for us to know him. We learn that he owns the cattle on a thousand hills (Ps 50:10-13) and can provide exceedingly, abundantly above all that we could ever imagine to ask from him (Eph 3:20). The more we know about who God is, the more we have both the desire and the confidence to come to him in prayer.

At the end of the parable, Jesus revealed that it was the host's persistence that drove the friend out of bed to procure the resources he requested (v. 8). The verbs Jesus used to describe the process of prayer reflect a perpetuation of action: keep asking, keep seeking, keep knocking. Praying continually in the manner Jesus taught aligns our hearts with the will of God. We acknowledge God's power and glory, praising him for who he is and thanking him for revealing himself to us. We surrender to his plans for our lives, believing that even challenging circumstances are for our good. We recognize our limited resources, relying on him for daily necessities (Lk 12:22-31). We confess our sin before him, admitting our desperate need for

The more we know about who God is, the more we have both the desire and the confidence to come to him in prayer.

Kingdom Fruits

his grace every hour and trusting him to deliver us fully and finally from evil through Christ. Aligning our hearts with God's will is a moment-by-moment process (1 Thes 5:17). Our hearts are quick to glory in ourselves or others, to trust in our own resources and plans, to despair in guilt or shame. Jesus' remedy to each and every need is to ask, seek, knock. When we delight in his will, we learn to desire his will; when we desire his will, God rises with joy to pour out the infinite resources of his presence and provision (Ps 37:4).

Day 27

Food for Thought
Read 1 John 5:14-15. Here, John describes the confidence we can have in God's promises to hear and answer prayers prayed in alignment with his will. Given such a glorious promise, what keeps you from praying without ceasing? Reflect on the source of any hesitations today. Do you feel that your wisdom and power are sufficient to maintain good circumstances? Do you feel ashamed to confess again to a holy God? Do you lack the faith to believe that he really hears you? In response to every possible hesitation, Jesus lovingly beckons: ask, seek, knock.

Faith in Action
Throughout the day, notice your heart's meditations. How often do you engage with God, actively aligning your will with his? Do you only look to him when you've exhausted all of your own resources? Practice seeking him moment-by-moment today. Ask for wisdom as you begin a conversation; thank God for daily provisions like health, food, and clothing; rehearse the grace he has poured out on you when you are tempted to criticize others; ask for favor as you start a task.

Prayer
As you practice praying without ceasing today, aligning your will with God's throughout the day, spend some focused time praying out loud, if you are able. Talk with God about your understanding of and feelings about prayer. Ask him to deepen your love for communing with him and to give you the faith to believe that he hears you and responds to you in love.

Persistent Friend Part Two

Luke 11:1-13

I'll never forget the night I got the call that my father had died suddenly of a heart attack. It was one of those moments when time stands still—when everything in the world keeps moving except for you. In those rare moments, the shock of disbelief engulfs you like a fog in August. You begin to stumble forward, but you can only see a couple of feet in front of you. And that fog can last for days, weeks, or years.

The thing I miss the most since Dad died is the easy companionship that we shared. We had many of the same interests, from fishing to the 49ers. We could reminisce and discuss our interests for hours, but, at the same time, we could ride in the car together without saying a word, simply enjoying each other's proximity. Even now, years later, my eyes grow misty just thinking about it. I loved my dad, and I know that he loved me. He demonstrated that to me for 47 years. With God's help, he laid the foundation upon which I've built my life, and nothing I could do or give would ever be enough to repay him for his investment in my life.

Jesus concluded the parable of the Persistent Friend by painting a comforting and confidence-building

Kingdom Fruits

A child need not prepare a formal speech before enjoying the company of a loving parent— no, to enjoy their presence, she need only enter into it with gladness.

picture of who it is that we come to when we pray to God. Jesus said, "What father among you if his son asks for a fish, will instead of a fish give him a serpent; or if he asks for an egg, will give him a scorpion? If you then, who are evil, know how to give good gifts to your children, how much more will the heavenly Father give the Holy Spirit to those who ask him (vv. 11-13)!"

Here, Jesus used the language of family to describe our relationship with God. I can totally identify with this illustration both as a son and as a father. My dad wasn't perfect, but he certainly knew how to give his kids good gifts. When we had legitimate needs, he always provided them: food, shelter, clothing, medical care. He also knew how to give us extra blessings like braces, camps, vacations, and Christian education—often at great personal sacrifice for Mom and him. What I remember with the most fondness, though, is not the material provision and blessings my Dad provided. It is our relationship, which grew out of his presence in my life and simple conversation. I loved talking with my Dad—I never had to be forced to do it. It was natural and wonderful. How I wish I could talk with him one more time in this world.

This is how God wants us to view our conversations with him. In Jesus' vision of prayer, a child asks a father, "May I have fish for lunch today, or perhaps an egg?" This is a picture of the ongoing dialogue between a parent and child. There will be moments for reflection on the day's events, for petitions and requests, and even for instruction and rebuke. The parent will ask questions about the child's feelings and wellbeing. The child will rest in the companionable silence of the parent. This is not the image of high church sacrament or theological education. It's the language of love and life and food and shelter and grace and peace. It's the language of companionship.

Day 28

Why, then, do we struggle in prayer as we so often do? One temptation, as we saw yesterday, is to view prayer merely as an insurance card to be used only in emergencies. In that case, we will fail to pray when circumstances are good and cut ourselves off from the joys of communing with God daily. Another temptation, especially for those who have been following Jesus for a long time, is to view prayer as a barometer for "how we're doing" as disciples. It is calculable in minutes spent, meetings attended, and journals filled. As we've seen throughout our study, once we begin comparing our performance to a measuring stick or to others, either guilt or pride will be close at hand.

Guilt sees the measuring stick and says, "I should really pray more." Guilt in prayer imagines that God's pleasure toward us rests on our performance. We picture a displeased, impatient God waiting by the phone. When we think about our sinful thoughts and actions throughout the day, we avoid praying until we can try to "clean up" a little bit. When we do pray, we're so burdened by how long it's been or how unworthy we feel to talk to God that we don't joyfully experience familial companionship with God. We avoid prayer all the more, adding guilt upon guilt.

If this tends to describe your prayer journey, think about a loving parent and a child. Because children are not perfect, they will make mistakes and, sometimes, will even make deliberate decisions to disobey to test the limits of their parents' authority and desires for their life. In those moments, does a loving parent reject the child, treat her with silence, forego her daily provisions, or sever her from their loving embrace? Far from it. The loving parent moves toward the child—instructing, teaching, disciplining—with a confirming embrace and comforting truth: "You are my child whom I love. I will never leave you; I am for you." Children who believe the love of their parent and trust the heart of their parent toward them need not fear to approach their

> *The good gift we are promised when we pray is not the affirmative answer to the prayer request but the very presence of God.*

Kingdom Fruits

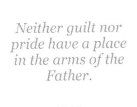

> *Neither guilt nor pride have a place in the arms of the Father.*

parent even when all is not well in their hearts and lives. In fact, when all is not well, they run faster and harder into the presence of their parent because there they find rest and help.

Pride equally cuts us off from companionable communion with God in prayer. Like guilt, pride in prayer also imagines that God's pleasure toward us waxes and wanes on the basis of our own performance as disciples. Pride sees a met benchmark like number of minutes per day or journal pages per week, and says, "I am doing great!" We can begin to boast inwardly in our own abilities, destructively devaluing God's grace in our heart of hearts. If we believe God's pleasure toward us mirrors our efforts in discipleship disciplines, it is a small step further to imagine that God's blessing toward us also depends on our performance. We may begin to believe that we can move God's hand to give us what we want or think we need, attributing blessings to the power of our own faith or obedience. If we pray as though our spiritual or material success rides on our own performance, then our burden is heavy, the striving is endless, and we, too, miss out on joyful communion with God.

If you tend to struggle with pride in prayer, imagine the joy of a loving parent surprising his children with a trip to Disney World. He loads the kids in the car without telling them where he's taking them. When they drive through the Magic Kingdom gates, they squeal with joy and begin to talk excitedly about all they will see and experience that day. The oldest child begins to fidget and mutter quietly about unfinished homework and chores. "Stop the car!" he finally cries out in a panic. "I'm sorry, but I just don't think we have been good enough this year to warrant a trip to Disney World. Maybe if we really follow through on everything you ask us to do next year and pool our allowances…" Imagine the parent's shock! The absurdity of the child's complaint is not in his desire to try to earn a

Day 28

gracious gift from his parent; our sinful nature wants to hold up our own merits as evidence of why we deserve gifts of grace. No, the absurdity is that the child has already entered Disney World. It's too late to go back home and craft a list of standards to meet in order to earn a trip to Disney World—the family is already through the gates.

In the same way, we can only come to God in prayer because he has *already* made a way for us to do so. It is not our performance but his that enables us to commune with the Father and enjoy the glorious benefits of his presence. It is the Father who adopted us as heirs to the glorious inheritance of his kingdom (Eph 1:3-6). It is the Holy Spirit who draws us to know and believe in the Father (Jn 16:7-15). It is Jesus' blood and intercession which grant us perpetual access to the Father (Rom 5:1-2, 8:34). Without God having *already* provided for our prayers, we would have no hope of entering his presence, speaking with him, or hearing from him. By his grace, he has provided for us in every way to come to him—not as a friendly neighbor who shares a little of his bread and wine when we ask, but as a Father who, in Christ, graciously gives us all things (Rom 8:32). Because he is our Father, we need not doubt our welcome. Because he is our Father, we need not strive to earn our keep. Neither guilt nor pride have a place in the arms of the Father.

Prayer is not manipulation or calculation. It is not a way to earn discipleship points. It is companionship. A child need not prepare a formal speech before enjoying the company of a loving parent—no, to enjoy their presence, she need only enter into it with gladness. When we do, God promises to meet us there. Note, again, Jesus' words in the parable: "If you then, who are evil, know how to give good gifts to your children, how much more will the heavenly Father give the *Holy Spirit* to those who ask him (v. 13, emphasis mine)!" The good gift we are promised when we pray is not the affirmative answer to the prayer request but the very presence of God. And, in his presence, there is "fullness of joy (Ps 16:11)." I wrote the song lyrics copied below in a moment of quiet companionship with the Fa-

Kingdom Fruits

ther. I hope they encourage you today to share your joys, sorrows, hopes, and hurts with God our Father in simple communion with him.

A Morning Prayer

Sovereign God, I bow to you today.
I give you every hope and fear.
Guide my steps, go before me,
Make your will, my will.

I need you, O my Father,
To feel the warmth of your embrace,
Reminding me that I'm your child;
And I'm covered by your grace.

Gracious God, I rest in you today.
I give you every care and tear.
Guard my heart, overwhelm me;
Make your love, my love.

I need you, O my Father,
To feel the warmth of your embrace,
Reminding me that I'm your child,
And I'm covered by your grace.

I need you.
I need you, Abba.

Day 28

Food for Thought

Read Matthew's account of Jesus' teachings on prayer in Mt 6:5-15. Notice his words in verse 7: "And when you pray, do not heap up empty phrases as the Gentiles do, for they think that they will be heard for their many words. Do not be like them, for your Father knows what you need before you ask him." Some use this verse to argue against the need for Christians to pray. But, in the next verse, Jesus said, "Pray then like this," and proceeded to teach the Lord's Prayer. Jesus' call is not to avoid prayer but rather to approach God as a loving Father who knows what we need and promises to welcome us into his presence. When we trust the Father's heart toward us, his children, we will delight to enter his presence in prayer.

Faith in Action

Our hearts are prone to forget the amazing grace of God who chose us, adopted us, and welcomed us into his presence. When we elevate our own performance, it is easy to feel the need to "heap up empty phrases" before God and others. We may try to show how much we know about God through our expertly-worded praises and requests. We may feel the need to put on a show. Doing so saps our enjoyment of God's fatherly presence. As you live in moment-by-moment awareness of God's presence today, actively remember your identity as God's child and enjoy the freedom to speak, listen, and rest in his companionship.

Prayer

As you pray today, imagine sitting out on your back steps with God just talking about your day, your dreams, and your fears. Tell him you love him and rehearse his love for you. Thank him for everything he has given you in Christ. As you worship, surrender, pray for provision, ask forgiveness, and give thanks for grace, do so like you would talk with a friend and Father. Enjoy being in God's presence. He not only promises to meet you in prayer—he delights to hear from you!

Faithful Servants

Luke 12:35-40

A dear sister in the Lord once shared with me how, right after their wedding, her husband enlisted to serve in World War II. He left immediately, promising to come back. She understood enough about war to know that he didn't have the power to guarantee that promise, but she did not lose hope that he would return. In fact, she waited by the window every day for as many minutes as she could spare. She imagined what he would look like walking up the road, turning into the yard, climbing the porch steps. She longed for him to come back, anticipating the joyous moment. Her active anticipation at the window demonstrated a hope-filled belief in her husband's return. In God's sovereign plan, one day, he did walk up the road, turn into the yard, and climb the porch steps. And, what a reunion it was!

Jesus knows everything about us, including our hearts' propensity to wander away from the window of anticipating his return. In Luke 12, Jesus instructed a crowd to lay up heavenly treasure, "For where your treasure is, there will your heart be also (Lk 12:34)." Then, he began today's parable: "Stay dressed for action and keep your lamps burning, and be like men who are waiting for their master to come home from the wedding feast, so that they

Kingdom Fruits

> Once we understand the hope of Jesus' return, we can't help but look with longing for his appearing.

may open the door to him at once when he comes and knocks (vv. 35-36)."

The language may be obscure, so let me set the scene. In Jesus' day, the owner of an estate would employ servants to care for it. Some would work inside, while others worked in the yard, barns, and fields. At night, the gate to the house would be locked in order to keep the family safe from thieves. Should the owner of the house go out for the evening, the gate would be guarded by his servants until he returned. In the absence of electricity, light was supplied with lanterns, which required oil and wicks. Both had to be tended continually to ensure that the flame didn't go out. Without the convenience of matches or butane lighters, relighting an oil lamp was no easy task. If the lanterns went out, the residents would be left in darkness.

The servants in Jesus' story had no way to communicate with their boss once he left the house, so they couldn't know for sure what time he would be home. He might be gone for a couple of hours or half the night. They needed to stay awake and alert so that when he returned and knocked at the gate they could give him swift entry. It was also critically important that the lamps be lit when he arrived. It was dangerous to be lingering in the darkness outside the gate in the middle of the night. Can you imagine the anger of the estate owner if he arrived home to find his gatekeepers asleep, with their lanterns cold and dark? It would not produce a positive outcome for the servants.

If, instead, the master found his servants awake and alert, he would be filled with joy over their good work. Jesus continued, "Blessed are those servants whom the master finds awake when he comes. Truly, I say to you, he will dress himself for service and have them recline at table, and he will come and serve them. If he comes in the second watch [9 PM], or in the third [midnight], and finds them awake, blessed are those servants (vv. 37-38)!" Rath-

Day 29

er than arriving to a dark and dangerous setting, the estate owner found his staff ready to open the door and welcome him back. He was so grateful that he planned an event just to serve and reward them for a job well done.

Jesus explained this parable in view of the eschaton – the end of the age. He said, "But know this, that if the master of the house had known at what hour the thief was coming, he would not have left his house to be broken into (v. 39)." Clearly, if the estate owner had known that his home was about to be broken into, he would have stayed home. In the same way, we do not know the appointed hour of Jesus' return; as a result, we must wait with vigilance, resisting spiritual slumber. Jesus concluded, "You also must be ready, for the Son of Man is coming at an hour you do not expect (v. 40)." With these words, Jesus reaches through the pages of history and taps each of us on the shoulder: "*You* also must be ready." 2,000 years have passed since Jesus ascended into heaven, and only God the Father knows (Mt 24:36) the day when Jesus will return just as he left (Acts 1:8-11). But, return he will, and he instructs us to wait faithfully – to be found dressed for action, awake, and alert.

The question for us is, how? What does faithful waiting look like, and how do we avoid spiritual slumber? Like the estate servants, we must first believe that our Master will fulfill his promise to return. If they did not believe that the master would return, they would be foolish to suffer the discomfort of staying awake and alert. Staying awake revealed their belief that the master would return. Second, we must live our lives with an ongoing expectation of the Master's promised return. Because the estate servants believed the owner's promise, they expected its fulfillment and acted accordingly. They watched the road for him. They kept the lamps lit. These actions in *anticipation* of the master's return

Jesus' promised return offers a bottomless well of peace from which to drink deeply in the midst of life's driest deserts.

Kingdom Fruits

> Jesus reaches through the pages of history and taps each of us on the shoulder: "You also must be ready."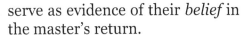

serve as evidence of their *belief* in the master's return.

In the same way, our actions serve as evidence of our belief in and anticipation of Jesus' promise to come again. Jesus told this parable in the context of our treasure. The young wife revealed her treasure by watching and waiting in the window. Had she ceased to believe her husband's promise to return, she would have wandered out in search of another occupation or love to fill the void. Christians who have fallen asleep to Christ's return similarly wander in pursuit of earth's passing treasures. Think of the person who can't imagine an afterlife and doesn't believe the soul persists into eternity. This person will approach life on earth as the only guarantee – a person's one shot at happiness and fullness. This person will naturally fight to preserve life at all costs, hoarding resources, prioritizing comfort, and idolizing safety. They will engage in an endless search for pleasure, people, or possessions that they hope will finally make them happy. Does this not remind you of your own heart's tendencies to clasp earth's meager offerings? This is the essence of falling asleep to Christ's return. In slumber, we wander from the window, forgetting what glorious hope and what eternal treasures are ours in his promise to come again.

My wife Lyla likes to read the back of the book to determine whether she wants to read the whole story. While, to me, this behavior entirely ruins the fun of fiction, I understand it from the standpoint of emotional investment. If the novel ends with the death of every beloved character, she may choose not to invest hours of her life into knowing and loving those characters. If, however, the ending reflects a joyous outcome for the protagonists, she can read the rest of the story with hope. When the rising conflict sees the characters suffering, she can endure the twists and turns with patience because she knows how the story ends.

Day 29

Because God has revealed to us the end of the story, we need not fear rising conflict in our lives or our world. Knowing the denouement changes everything about how we experience the rest of the story. When we believe Jesus' promise to return and reign with perfect justice and love, we can endure the suffering and injustice we experience in our sin-shattered world.

Let us not live as those who have no hope, fixated on what meager possessions and positions we can obtain in this short life.

When we believe that he will restore all that has been broken by sin, we can look on our fellow humans with compassion, extending mercy to those who need it as we ourselves do. When we believe that he will establish a New Heaven and New Earth, we can loosen our grip on earth's passing possessions. Jesus' promised return offers a bottomless well of hope from which to drink deeply in the midst of life's driest deserts. This is why Jesus commands us to stay awake to his return. In view of our glorious future, we can't help but look with longing for his appearing. We can't help but anticipate the fulfillment of these promises, and this anticipation changes how we live while we wait.

Jesus told us to be ready. We cannot know the day he will return, but we can trust his promise. Let us not live as those who have no hope, fixated on what meager possessions and positions we can obtain in this short life. Let us not be lulled back to sleep by the comforts of what we can see and grasp. Let us, instead, pray for more faith to believe Jesus' promise to return. Let us pray for the Spirit-empowered expectation to keep a steadfast watch at the window.

Kingdom Fruits

Food for Thought We saw today how falling asleep to Christ's return can lead us to tighten our grip on earthly kingdoms and sever us from true hope. Read 2 Peter 3, and reflect on your vision of eternity today. Are you allowing the end of the story to influence how you are living in the middle? If we believe God's revelation of Jesus' return is true, Peter asks, "What sort of people ought you to be in lives of holiness and godliness, waiting for and hastening the coming of the day of God (vv. 11-12)?" Allow the Holy Spirit to reveal how you are waiting for Christ's return.

Faith in Action In 2 Peter 3, Peter said that in the last days some will assume that Jesus is never coming back. How does he explain God's perception of time as different than our own? In verse 9, Peter explains that God's apparent delay is actually patience toward his children who have yet to "reach repentance." While we long for and live in the hope of Jesus' return, let us also thank him for his delay, remembering those in our lives who have yet to repent and believe. Today, look for opportunities to share the hope that you have with those who do not yet know God.

Prayer
As you pray today, talk with God about how difficult it is to live with an anticipation of Christ's return. Share with him the earthly concerns that tempt you to live as if this life is all that is promised. Ask him to help you live in the hope-giving reality of his return, to keep your lantern lit, and to stay awake and alert in your spiritual life. Finally, pray for the return of Jesus in light of 2 Peter 3.

Day 30

Persistent Widow

Luke 18:1-8

Our world is filled with injustice. Almost daily we hear the stories: the woman who loses custody of her children because her ex-husband has the money to hire a good attorney; the employees who lose their pensions because unethical people have mismanaged it; the murderer released from prison on a technicality; the child kidnapped by traffickers for the sex trade; the people who starve under the evil regimes of dictators; the innocent people who suffer persecution for their Christian faith.

When we hear about these situations, something in our spirit groans within us. Intuitively, we understand that these things are wrong and have no place in our world. What is the source of this universal emotion? It certainly isn't naturalism and its evolutionary processes. There is no sense of justice in the animal kingdom—might makes right. And if, as some say, we're simply more highly evolved animals, then we shouldn't have a notion of justice either. Yet, we do. The desire for justice is a universal one because we are created in the image of God (Gen 1:26-27). God is just (Rom 12:19), and as image-bearers of God, we are called to desire and demonstrate that justice to others (Micah 6:8). Whether we acknowledge it or not, our desire for justice is rooted in the fact that we bear the image of a God who is just.

Kingdom Fruits

> The desire for justice is a universal one because we are created in the image of God.

In today's parable, Jesus tells a story about injustice toward one of society's most vulnerable populations: widows. Jesus began, "In a certain city there was a judge who neither feared God nor respected man (v. 2)." Judges are uniquely positioned either to dispense justice or to disregard it. In this instance, the judge was unconcerned about justice. He didn't fear God, who had both given the law and dictated the way it should be administered. Neither did he respect humanity as image-bearers of God, deserving of justice. Instead, he placed his own comfort and financial well-being ahead of those he was supposed to serve. For him, "justice" went to the highest bidder, and business was good.

Enter the widow. Jesus said of her, "And there was a widow in that city who kept coming to him and saying, 'Give me justice against my adversary (v. 3).'" From this statement, we learn that the widow had been wronged. Perhaps someone had swindled her out of her house or land (Micah 2:2, 9) or had taken advantage of her in business, robbing her of money that was rightfully hers (Micah 6:9-11). Regardless of the reason, the widow had been wronged, and she wanted it put right. We also learn that she was persistent. Notice the words "kept coming to him." Undaunted, the widow went before the judge frequently in her pursuit of justice.

Eventually, the judge became fatigued by her presence. Jesus said, "For a while he refused, but afterward he said to himself, 'Though I neither fear God nor respect man, yet because this widow keeps bothering me, I will give her justice, so that she will not beat me down by her continual coming (vv. 4-5).'" As you can see, the judge was unconcerned about her situation. Initially, he refused to help her. Perhaps she was in a dispute with one of his family members or friends. Maybe the political leaders had played a role in her situation. Regardless, he was easily persuaded to rule against her. He didn't care what God

Day 30

thought about her situation or how his ruling would affect her. It was business as usual.

Until it wasn't. The widow just wouldn't go away and take no for an answer. Over and over, she showed up at the city gate demanding justice. While a mere nuisance at first, over time it would have become an embarrassment to the judge. Every time this humble widow demanded justice, she highlighted the fact that the judge was crooked. He knew he was crooked, of course, but he still didn't enjoy having it put on display. Eventually, it was going to be bad for business. So the judge made a strategic decision: he would give her justice so that she would stop "beating him down by her continual coming." Finally, justice in hand, the widow went about her business.

Having told the parable, Jesus explained it. "Hear what the unrighteous judge says. And will not God give justice to his elect, who cry to him day and night? Will he delay long over them? I tell you, he will give justice to them speedily (vv. 6-7)." We need to pause at this point to understand the identities of the characters in the parable. Though Jesus compares God's justice toward his children to the crooked judge's eventual judgment in favor of the widow, the crooked judge in this parable is not a representation of God. God does not wield judgment as an instrument for personal gain. He is perfectly just, meaning he cannot be anything but wholly righteous in his judgments. He knows the deepest recesses of every heart and understands every motivation, thought, and deed (Heb 4:12-13); he always knows the whole story. Jesus asks, in essence, if even a corrupt judge will eventually abandon corruption to exercise justice toward the persistent widow, how much more will a wholly just God exercise swift and righteous justice on behalf of his children?

The second character is the widow, and she is a representation of suffering Christians who long for justice to come. Because we

Because we live in a world that has been broken and poisoned by the effects of sin, we will experience injustice.

205

Kingdom Fruits

> The justice of God gives us hope for a future in which every wrong will be made right.

live in a world that has been broken and poisoned by the effects of sin, we will experience injustice. We will be misunderstood, misbelieved, lied to, and lied about. We will see one set of rules applied to us, and another set of rules applied to someone else. We will witness others cheat and seem to get ahead, free of consequences. At times, as we battle our sin nature, we will even perpetrate injustice toward another. In those times, whether we face injustice or become aware of our own, what keeps us from despairing? Our hope is that our God is just.

God's just nature gives us hope for the injustice we experience and the injustice we find in our own hearts. First, we need not despair of the injustice we find in our own hearts. A right understanding of the gospel of Jesus Christ reminds us that our sin, including our unfair biases and wrongful treatment of others, has been defeated at the cross. There, Jesus took upon himself the deserved punishment for our corrupt motivations, thoughts, and behaviors. When those whom we've wronged demand cosmic punishment for our wickedness, we need only point to the cross and hold up hands that have been washed clean by the blood of Jesus. Yes, God has rightly judged our sin, but he meted out the punishment to his own Son on our behalf, and so, we are not condemned (Rom 8:1). This is cause for great rejoicing in the justice of God.

Second, God's just nature means we need not despair over injustice we experience at the hands of others because no wicked deed will go unpunished. If we suffer at the hands of another child of God, we can be confident that Jesus already paid the righteous price for that specific sin against us. God's wrath was poured out against that wickedness to the fullest extent of the law. We can also be confident that in his time and way, God will convict their spirits or execute loving discipline in their lives to bring them back to right fellowship with him. He loves us too much to allow us to sit comfortably in sin (Heb 12:5-11).

When we suffer injustice at the hands of those who are not children of God, our hope remains the same. No wicked deed will go unpunished. Without the interposed blood of Jesus, the unjust will pay the righteous price for their own sin. God's wrath will be poured out on their wickedness to the fullest extent of the law, and they will experience eternity separated from God and every shadow of his goodness and grace. Because God is just, we can be confident that justice will win in the end. This is great cause for rejoicing because we are, therefore, freed from any need to exact vengeance, hold grudges, or feel hatred toward those who wrong us, each of which robs us of abiding in and enjoying Christ.

How then do we respond to injustice? The beginning of today's parable gives us the answer: "And he told them a parable to the effect that they ought always to pray and not lose heart (v. 1)." In response to our own tendencies toward injustice, we should pray and not lose heart. As we daily abide in Christ, we should ask for eyes to see our own crooked thoughts and deeds. Christians who are in step with the Spirit will grieve when convicted of injustice, but we must not lose heart. Instead, we must repent and run to Jesus for mercy again and again. We must turn from our sin in the power of the Spirit, desiring to become more and more like Jesus. And, we must rehearse the glorious truth that Jesus paid it all.

In response to the injustice we experience, we should likewise pray and not lose heart. As we daily abide in Christ, we will experience suffering in this world. Jesus said, "In the world you *will* have tribulation (Jn 16:33, emphasis mine)." Seeking God's kingdom first is an act of war against the "cosmic powers over this present darkness (Eph 6:12)." We should expect to endure not only inconvenient injustices at the hands of others, but also hatred, persecution, and suffering (Jn 15:18-25). Jesus described what we can expect when we follow him: "Then they will deliver you up to tribulation and put you to death, and you

Kingdom Fruits

will be hated by all nations for my name's sake. And then many will fall away and betray one another and hate one another (Mt 24:9-10)."

This is a bleak picture. And, yet, Jesus tells us to take heart. Do not despair, he says, for "I have overcome the world (Jn 16:33)." The justice of God gives us hope for a future in which every wrong will be made right. Seeing and suffering injustice causes us rightly to lament, but one day, every last tear will be wiped away (Rev 21:3-4), and true justice will reign for all eternity (Rev 22:1-5). When we live with that sure future in view, we access the power to take heart in the face of every form of injustice, and we access the power to pray. For those who persecute us (Lk 6:27-28), for endurance through suffering, and for more faith to believe God's promise that "after you have suffered a little while, the God of all grace, who has called you to his eternal glory in Christ, will himself restore, confirm, strengthen, and establish you. To him be the dominion forever and ever. Amen (1 Pet 5:10-11)."

Day 30

Food for Thought One of the most popular verses in Christendom is Romans 8:28, which says, "And we know that for those who love God all things work together for good, for those who are called according to his purpose." How does our study of God's justice today inform our understanding and application of that verse? Read Romans 8:12-30 and note the future-oriented context. God may choose to make some wrongs right in the here and now to accomplish his kingdom purposes, but our hope for all things working together is in the promise of a glorious future with our Just God.

Faith in Action God's justice enables us to forgive those who treat us unfairly, wrong us, or persecute us and frees us from guilt and shame over the injustices we have committed. Reflect on your heart today; are you holding onto hurts, hoping for vengeance for those who've wronged you? Take time to rehearse the outcome of those sins against you in light of God's perfect justice. Are you gripped by guilt and shame? Take time to rehearse what God's justice means for the sins you have committed. Because God is just, he could never exact another payment for sins, great or small, for which Jesus has already paid the full price. This is cause for great rejoicing even in the midst of suffering.

Prayer Jesus tells us to pray and not to lose heart. In light of injustice, it is right for us to lament and cry out to God to make broken things whole. It is right to pray for Spirit-powered endurance through suffering. Do so today over the injustice you see, experience, and perpetrate. Our Father hears our cries and will establish perfect justice. Ask for eyes to see the hope that God's justice affords us in this life and the next.

Finding L.I.F.E. in Jesus!

Everyone wants to be happy. The hard part is determining exactly what that means. For some, happiness is defined through relationships. They believe that popularity, a huge friend list on Facebook, and a significant other produces happiness. For others, happiness is defined through success. They believe that personal achievement, a huge number in their bank account, and plenty of expensive toys produces happiness. For still others, happiness is defined through community. They believe that personal growth, impacting societal change, and embracing diversity produces happiness. And these things do—until they don't.

Finding happiness is one of the most difficult things in life. Often, it appears to be right in front of us, but then it slips through our fingers and is gone. Friends, achievement, and personal growth have the potential to bring happiness into our lives, but when our friends disappear, success eludes us, and we realize that we're incapable of self–transformation, happiness is quickly replaced by disillusionment and depression. The problem with pursuing happiness is that it is an emotion that is driven by our circumstances. And let's be honest—we all tend to have more negative than positive experiences in our lives.

So, what's the answer? Should we keep doing the same things while expecting different results, or should we consider what Jesus has to say about finding our purpose for life? If you want to stay on the hamster wheel while you try to catch up to happiness, you can stop reading here. But if you're ready to consider what God wants to do in your life, please read on.

God never promises happiness in the Bible. Are you surprised to hear that? Instead, he promises something much greater—joy. While happiness is an emotion fueled by circumstance, joy is an attitude fueled by God's Spirit. Happiness is self–determined. In other words, I am the sole determiner of whether I'm happy at any given moment. Joy, on the other hand, is God–determined. God has promised to give us joy, and it isn't based on our circumstances—it's based on God's character and promises.

This is why Jesus never talks about giving people happiness. He knew all too well that chasing happiness is like chasing your shadow. You can never catch it. Instead, he talks about giving people life. He said, "I came that they may have life and have it abundantly (Jn 10:10)." Here, Jesus reveals that the thing people really want, whether they know it or not, is abundant life. To have an abundant life means that you are personally satisfied in all areas of your life, and you experience peace and contentment as a result. Jesus' statement also means that we do not have the capacity to create that kind of life for ourselves. Jesus came in order to give it to us. But how? The Bible tells us that achieving this kind of satisfied life requires us to know something about God, ourselves, and the reason for the death and resurrection of Jesus Christ.

First, we must understand God's **love**. The Bible says that God is love (I Jn 4:8), and God created us so that we could know him and experience his love (Gen 1:26–31). God created us to be worshipers and to live forever in the reality of his glory. And, when sin marred his perfect creation, he created a plan to free men and women from its curse. At just the right time in history, God sent his own Son, Jesus, into our world. "For God so loved the

Finding L.I.F.E. in Jesus!

world, that he gave his only Son, that whoever believes in him should not perish but have eternal life (Jn 3:16)." It is God's love that motivates him to restore relationship with those who are separated from him by sin.

Second, we must understand our **isolation**. To be isolated is to be separated from someone, and as a result, to be alone. This is what sin has done to us. It has separated us from the very one we were created to know, love, and worship—God. When Adam and Eve rebelled against God by breaking the lone command he had given them, the entire world was brought under the curse of sin (Gen 3). As a result, God removed them from the Garden of Eden, and their perfect fellowship with God was broken. In an instant, they had become isolated from God because of their sin. From that moment to this, every person born into this world is guilty of sin. The Bible says, "For all have sinned and fall short of the glory of God (Rom 3:23)." Because of this "there is none righteous, no, not one (Rom 3:10)." Further, "The wages of sin is death (Rom 6:23a)." We were created to love and worship God in perfect community, but now because of sin we are isolated from him. Meanwhile, we try to satisfy this desire to know God by pursuing our own happiness, even though we can never hope to attain it. And in doing so, we risk being isolated from God for all eternity.

Third, we must understand our need for **forgiveness.** There is only one way to experience God's love and escape the isolation caused by sin—we must experience God's forgiveness. In spite of sin, God never stopped loving the people he created. He promised Adam and Eve that he would send someone who could fix the problem they had created. When it was time, God sent his own Son, Jesus, to be the world's Savior. This, too, was an act of God's love. The Bible says, "God shows his love for us in that while we were still sinners, Christ died for us (Rom 5:8)." When Jesus died on the cross, he was paying the penalty for our sins (Rom 3:23–26). When God raised Jesus from the dead, it was to demonstrate that forgiveness was available to all who would receive it by faith. Paul explained how this happens in his letter to the Ephesians. "For by grace you have been saved through faith. And this is not your own doing; it is the gift of God, not a result of works, so that no one may boast (Eph 2:8–9)."

The reality is that we cannot experience salvation as a result of our own efforts. We can try to be a good person, go to a church, even give a ton of money to worthy causes—none of these "works" can provide forgiveness. No matter how hard we try, we will always "fall short of the glory of God." That is why we must receive God's offer of forgiveness and salvation by faith. Faith simply means to trust or believe. Salvation requires us to believe that God loves us, that we are isolated from him by our sins, and that his Son Jesus died and was raised to life again to pay the sin debt that we owe God because of our sins. When we take God up on his offer of the gift of salvation, he doesn't just give us forgiveness—he gives us life! The Bible says, "The free gift of God is eternal life in Christ Jesus our Lord (Rom 6:23)."

Fourth, we must understand the **enjoyment** that comes from knowing, loving, and worshiping God. Whether we know it or not, we are slaves to sin until God sets us free (Rom 6:20–23). This was the ultimate reason that God sent his Son, Jesus, to die on the cross for our sins—God sent Jesus so that we could be set free from our sins. Jesus said, "You will know the truth, and the truth will set you free. . . . Everyone who commits sin is a slave to sin. . . . So, if the Son sets you free, you will be free indeed (Jn 8:32–36)." Jesus was teaching us that we must be set free from sin in order to enjoy the life that God has given us—both now and in eternity future. We are set free when we commit our lives to Jesus Christ through faith in his death and resurrection. Then, and only then, will we find joy in the abundant life of Jesus Christ!

So, the question for you is a simple one: Are you ready to experience freedom from sin and the abundant life that Jesus promised you? If so, God is waiting for you to talk with him about it (Jer 29:13). Stop right where you are and make this your prayer to God,

Finding L.I.F.E. in Jesus!

"Father in heaven, I know that I'm a sinner. I know that I've done lots of things that displease you and disappoint you. And, I know that I'm isolated from you because of my sin. I know that if I die without knowing you, I will spend forever separated from you in hell. But, I believe that Jesus is your sinless Son, and I believe that he died on the cross for me. I believe that he died to provide a perfect payment for my sin debt. I believe that you raised him from the dead so that I could experience forgiveness for my sins. Right now, Father, I'm asking you to forgive me of my sins and save me. I am receiving your Son Jesus as my personal Lord and Savior. I will follow you the rest of my life. Please give me the joy of a life spent knowing, loving, and worshiping you. I ask these things in Jesus' name, Amen."

If you made the decision to accept Jesus as your Savior today, we want to talk with you! Please contact the people at www.seed-publishing-group.com. We would love to talk with you about your decision and help you with your first steps in following Jesus!

If you enjoyed *30 Days to The Parables*, check out the other books in the *30 Days to the Bible* series.

30 Days to Genesis

30 Days to Deuteronomy

30 Days to Ruth/Esther

30 Days to 1 Samuel

30 Days to Jeremiah/Lamentations

30 Days to John

30 Days to Acts

30 Days to James

Looking for an amazing discipleship tool for your church? Consider, *Aspire: Transformed by the Gospel*. This practical resource, written in two parts by Dr. Matt Rogers, will provide your church with a reproducible model that will turn your members into disciples who make disciples. Here is how the process works:

- Book One: A 14-week study of God's redemptive plan as revealed through the Bible. Beginning in Genesis, this study will reveal the redemptive themes of scripture, which culminate in the death and resurrection of Jesus.

- Book Two: A 15-week study of the implications of the Gospel for daily Christian living. This books reveals the way the Gospel impacts one's understanding of issues like worship, character, the work of the Holy Spirit, spiritual gifts, prayer, evangelism, stewardship, and marriage and family.

Taken together, these two volumes will take your people to a new level of discipleship and engagement with the scriptures and the local church. Churches across the US are utilizing this model with great affect. You should consider it too!